THE BEST OF
BIRDS & BLOOMS

contents

18
The World
of Birdsongs

from the editor

Another year is here! So grab a cup of coffee, sit back and enjoy the latest edition of *The Best of Birds & Blooms*. This essential resource is packed from cover to cover with interesting features, clever backyard projects and inspirational ideas from the past year of *Birds & Blooms* magazine. Readers and experts alike share their stories, photos, advice and tips for birders and gardeners just like you.

Discover the amazing wildlife tours that make bird-watching even more of an adventure in "The Trip of a Lifetime" (page 172). Read "Diary of a Monarch" (page 214) to follow this fascinating butterfly on its incredible annual journey. And learn how to transform the shady areas of your yard into a rainbow of flowering color in "The Bright Side of Shade" (page 140).

That's just a sample of everything that awaits you in this edition of *The Best of Birds & Blooms*. It's a collection every outdoor enthusiast is sure to appreciate now and for years to come.

Stacy Tornio

Editor, *Birds & Blooms*

bring solar to your garden (page 98) in less than an hour!

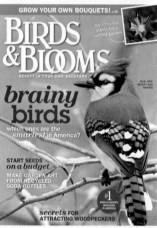

COVERS (THIS PAGE, TOP TO BOTTOM): CHICKADEE, BLUE JAY: MASLOWSKI WILDLIFE; BLUEBIRD, NORTHERN FLICKER: MARIE READ (LEFT, TOP TO BOTTOM); GOLDFINCH: MARIE READ; NUTHATCH: FUSE/GETTYIMAGES.COM; HUMMINGBIRD: TIM FITZHARRIS; WARBLER: MARIE READ; (RIGHT, TOP TO BOTTOM) GOLDFINCH: STEVE & DAVE MASLOWSKI; MONARCH: WALLY EBERHART/GETTY IMAGES; WOODPECKER, OWL: MARIE READ; FACING PAGE (LEFT, TOP TO BOTTOM): GOLDFINCH: MARIE READ

EDITORIAL
Editor-In-Chief Catherine Cassidy
Creative Director Howard Greenberg
Editorial Operations Director Kerri Balliet

Managing Editor/Print & Digital Books Mark Hagen
Associate Creative Director Edwin Robles Jr.

Editors Michelle Rozumalski, Amy Glander
Associate Editor Molly Jasinski
Art Director Raeann Sundholm
Layout Designer Nancy Novak
Editorial Production Manager Dena Ahlers
Copy Chief Deb Warlaumont Mulvey
Copy Editor Dulcie Shoener
Contributing Copy Editor Valerie Phillips

Editor, *Birds & Blooms* Stacy Tornio
Associate Creative Director, *Birds & Blooms* Sharon K. Nelson

BUSINESS
Vice President, Publisher Russell S. Ellis
Associate Marketing Director, Integrated Solutions Katie Gaon
Vice President, Brand Marketing Jennifer Smith
Vice President, Circulation & Continuity Marketing Dave Fiegel

READER'S DIGEST NORTH AMERICA
Vice President, Business Development & Marketing Alain Begun
President, Books & Home Entertainment Harold Clarke
General Manager, Canada Philippe Cloutier
Vice President, Operations Mitch Cooper
Vice President, Chief Marketing Officer Leslie Doty
Chief Operating Officer Howard Halligan
Vice President, Chief Sales Officer Mark Josephson
Vice President, Digital Sales Steve Sottile
Vice President, Chief Content Officer Liz Vaccariello
Vice President, Global Financial Planning & Analysis Devin White

THE READER'S DIGEST ASSOCIATION, INC.
President and Chief Executive Officer Robert E. Guth
@2014 Reiman Media Group, Inc.
5400 S. 60th St., Greendale WI 53129

International Standard Book Number: 978-1-61765-271-4

International Standard Serial Number: 1553-8400

Pictured on the front cover:
American goldfinch, Steve & Dave Maslowski
Bordered patch butterfly on blanket flower,
Rolf Nussbaumer/rolfnnp.com

Pictured on the back cover:
Hummingbird, Lance Bruce
Liatris, Mae Dricken
Monarchs on sunflower, Patty Jennings

the best in
Bird-Watching

Discover fascinating new facts about your favorite feeder visitors. Learn more about those elusive species you have yet to encounter. Share in the amazing experiences of bird-watching enthusiasts just like you.

TERRY A. PARKER/GETTY IMAGES

it starts with a
spark

A single moment can ignite a lifetime of bird-watching.

BY KEN KEFFER

Do you remember the moment you were first fully captivated by nature? Can you pinpoint the split second that changed you from a casual observer to someone with a true passion for the outdoors?

Many of us have had a lifelong love of nature, but there's usually a point in time that stands out in our memories. This is our spark moment.

While spark moments can happen with all things natural, the concept is especially popular with birders. A spark bird doesn't have to be rare to have an appeal. Many people admit that they never paid much attention to birds, overlooking even the most abundant ones, until their spark moment captured them.

My own spark bird tale is quite atypical. When I was a teenager, a beautiful bird caught my attention. What makes my story unusual is that I didn't actually see the bird itself.

I was hiking at a youth conservation camp in the Wind River Mountains of Wyoming. At the trailhead I noticed a sign with a picture of a duck on it. I assumed the duck was a rare species because the sign said the state game and fish department was interested in sightings.

I'd been duck hunting with my dad, but I'd never seen a duck that looked quite like that one. It was slate gray with vibrant rusty sides and bold white markings along the head and body. I thought it was stunning.

During the rest of the week, I was distracted by thoughts of that duck.

Though I didn't find one on that trip, my spark had been ignited. For the first time ever, birds were on my radar—and at that moment I became a birder. The experience even shaped my future career, pushing me toward the field of wildlife biology.

I spent the next decade searching for the dapper harlequin, but I didn't see this magnificent duck until just a few winters ago off the Rhode Island coast. It was a special moment, a culmination of the 11 years since I had first spotted that sign in the Wyoming wilderness.

Spark birds may be flashy, like yellow goldfinches, blue buntings and bright red cardinals, or they may be relatively plain, fading into the background. Perhaps it's an interesting

real spark birds

Enjoy these experiences from birding celebrities and readers to learn how they got hooked on birds.

LAURA ERICKSON
Author and
Naturalist
Duluth, Minnesota

JEFFREY GORDON
President of the
American Birding
Association
Colorado Springs,
Colorado

RACHEL BUTEK
2010 Young Birder
of the Year
Colfax, Wisconsin

My spark bird was actually a dead one, lying feet up on a sidewalk in downtown Chicago in 1968. It was exquisite, a tragic yet beautiful mystery: a tiny bird with an olive-brown back, white underside with black spots, white eye rings and an orange cap outlined with black. A few years later my mother-in-law gave me a field guide for Christmas, and I opened it right to the page with the ovenbird. This little book was my passport to a whole new world, and that ovenbird sparked a lifetime of love for birds.

In 1977, I was looking at the birds visiting our feeders, something I'd been doing casually for years. I knew the regular visitors—house finches, towhees, nuthatches and so on. And of course I knew goldfinches. I knew they were yellow in the spring and duller in the fall, and that the females were heavily streaked below. But that day, while looking in my field guide, it hit me: Those streaky birds I'd seen weren't goldfinches at all. They were pine siskins. The sense of discovery I felt was electric. At that moment, I became a birder.

The bird that truly sparked my interest was one special song sparrow. If I had known it was a song sparrow, it might not have made a difference. The intrigue of the unknown drew me to an old field guide. I waded through the pages of sparrows and finally identified my quarry. I was tickled to find something so delightful right outside my window! That childlike delight at discovering something new still drives my birding today.

behavior that catches your eye, or maybe a friend helps you identify a species for the first time. No matter the scene, spark moments are life-changing events. These birds ignite curiosity and fuel the desire to learn more about nature.

If you haven't met your spark bird yet, don't worry. It'll come when you're ready. And until then, you'll sure have a lot of fun looking!

FINDING YOUR SPARK.
Spark birds can be elusive, like Ken's harlequin duck (left), or common species like chickadees (above).

JEN ST. LOUIS
Elmira, Ontario

I went a little nuts when I heard reports of snowy owls in our area. Not 20 minutes into our search for them, we saw a female. That started my obsession with bird photography. I began planning my feeders and gardens according to what birds I could attract to our yard. To date, we've hosted 59 species!

SHARON SAURIOL
Macomb, Michigan

Chickadees always visit my feeders. They chatter so sweetly and are not afraid to come close to me. One day I held out my hand with a small piece of walnut in it. I was surprised when I felt the sweetest little peck as one of the chickadees took the treat right from my fingertips. This experience changed things for me, and I have been a birder ever since.

TIFFANY HAWKINS
Porter Ranch,
California

One spring afternoon I looked out the window at my new bird feeder and saw a strange visitor, which I eventually learned was a house finch. That bird opened up a whole new world to me. Bird-watchers have a term for birds that they see for the first time: lifers. Although my life list has since grown to 299 species, the most important lifer I ever saw was that little house finch. It truly was a life-changing bird.

bring on the
bluebirds

Here's how to double your chances of attracting these cheery charmers, *and* keep them around.

BY KENN AND KIMBERLY KAUFMAN

It's easy to see why eastern, western and mountain bluebirds are among the most beloved backyard visitors. With their gorgeous colors, musical voices and gentle habits, who wouldn't want to welcome these beauties into the backyard?

Attracting them can take some time and patience. But once you've won them over, they'll bring their special bluebird pizzazz to any yard or garden. Over the years, we've fielded hundreds of questions about bluebirds. So we thought we'd share a few of the most frequent ones and provide answers to help you see blue in no time.

A male bluebird (right) perches with a female holding nesting material.

Q: Is my yard a suitable habitat for bluebirds?

A: Bluebirds prefer open to semiopen areas. They feed mainly on insects, often watching from a low perch and then fluttering down to take bugs from the ground. A wide expanse of open, chemical-free lawn provides ideal habitat. A very small yard or one with little or no open space will probably not be suitable for nesting bluebirds.

Q: Are bluebirds endangered?

A: Bluebird populations are directly linked to human behavior. In the early 20th century, loss of habitat and competition for nesting cavities with the more aggressive house sparrows and European starlings had the species in serious decline. Fortunately, humans came to the rescue when bird enthusiasts realized these beauties were in trouble. Building nest boxes for them became a popular hobby, and the species began to rebound. Populations are now much more stable—and with our continued support, there's no reason bluebirds shouldn't grace our lives for generations to come.

Q: What kind of nest box should I buy or build?

A: A number of good designs are available, but remember that you must be able to open the box for routine nest checks and maintenance. If you're building your own, check with the North American Bluebird Society, *nabluebirdsociety.org*, for dimensions, and be sure to use a durable wood, such as cedar.

Q: What do I do about other birds using my bluebird boxes?

A: Bluebirds are cavity nesters. Instead of excavating their own nest holes, they use natural cavities in trees, abandoned holes made by woodpeckers, and man-made (and woman-made!) nest boxes. Several cavity-nesting birds will use bluebird boxes, which is fine as long as the nester is a member of a native species. (In fact, it's illegal to remove the nest of any native species.) Nonnatives are a different story. House sparrows, for instance, are very aggressive competitors for nesting space and will even kill bluebirds and other natives. So if you're not prepared to evict house sparrows from your boxes, being a bluebird landlord may not be for you.

Q: Where do my bluebirds go in winter?

A: Bluebirds disappear from many neighborhoods in winter, and it's natural to assume that they've all gone south, but this may not be the case. Some regularly stay through the winter as far north as Oregon, the southern Great Lakes and New England. They may switch habitats, however, gathering in small flocks and moving into open woods or juniper groves where wild fruits and berries will keep them fed in the cold. During the winter, small groups may roost together at night in tree holes or in other shelters. This is one good reason to consider leaving your nest boxes up for the winter season.

Q: I see a new nest in my bluebird box, but I don't see the parents. How can I tell if it's a bluebird nest?

A: Here's a quick guide to identifying the nests of some of the most likely species you'll find in your bluebird nest box.
EASTERN, MOUNTAIN AND WESTERN BLUEBIRD: Cup nest made of fine grasses and sometimes pine needles; eggs pale blue (rarely, pure white).
TREE SWALLOW: Cup nest of dried grass, always lined with feathers; eggs pure white.
HOUSE WREN: Nest made entirely of small twigs; eggs clear white, heavily speckled with reddish dots.
TITMOUSE: Cup nest of roots, moss and dried leaves lined with hair, fur and scraps of string and cloth; eggs creamy white, speckled with small dots.
CHICKADEE: Nest lined with moss, feathers, hair, rabbit fur and plant fiber; eggs white, evenly spotted.
NUTHATCH: Cup made with bark shreds, twigs, grasses, moss and feathers; eggs white, heavily speckled with pale brown or purplish spots.
HOUSE SPARROW: Unkempt domed nest often with scraps of trash; eggs greenish white, splotched gray and brown.

There'll be bluebirds over the white cliffs of Dover, Tomorrow, just you wait and see.
—NAT BURTON

An adult bluebird feeds a juvenile on a bright summer day.

Bluebird eggs are pale blue.

7 ways to make your yard more bluebird friendly.

1. OPEN IT UP. Bluebirds prefer open areas with low grass and perches from which they can hunt insects.

2. LEAVE IT ALONE. Dead trees provide important nesting and roosting sites for bluebirds and a whole host of other cavity-nesting birds. Leave dead trees standing (or leave dead limbs on live trees) when it's safe to do so.

3. PLANT NATIVE. In winter, bluebirds add berries and other fruit to their diet, so planting trees and shrubs native to your area is a natural way to attract them.

4. JUST ADD WATER. A simple birdbath is often enough, but bluebirds are partial to moving water, so a small fountain or dripper will make your water feature more enticing.

5. GO CHEMICAL-FREE. Between spring and fall, a bluebird's diet consists mainly of insects gleaned from the ground. Pesticides and other lawn chemicals are dangerous for birds that feed this way.

6. BEWARE OF ROAMING CATS. Every year, cats kill millions of songbirds. Newly fledged nestlings are especially vulnerable, so be a good bird landlord and keep your cats indoors.

7. OFFER MEALWORMS. Feeding live mealworms can pose some challenges, but bluebirds find them irresistible, even eating them from people's hands.

As you can see from this bluebird pair, they prefer open areas where they can perch and look for insects to eat.

bluebird bliss

These harbingers of spring bring a welcome case of the "blues."

BY GEORGE HARRISON, CONTRIBUTING EDITOR

Fifty years ago, the annual return of bluebirds—especially eastern bluebirds—to northern states in March signaled the much anticipated arrival of warmer weather.

With milder winters during the past couple of decades, many bluebirds now spend winters in their nesting areas all across the North. Still, the notes of the bluebird's first *tru-al-ly, tru-al-ly* warble are among the most welcome sounds of spring. And the bird's handsome colors—velvety sky blue on its back and shoulders, with an earthy, reddish-brown breast—are a visual treat.

A week or two after the male arrives, the female appears. Then, to the accompaniment of his own incessant warbling, the male pursues his chosen mate from one perch to another, often showing her areas available for nesting.

That's my cue to fill a tray feeder with live mealworms purchased from a local pet store. In my experience, placing the feeder in the vicinity of the birdhouses encourages bluebirds to nest there.

Making a Comeback

In the early to mid-1900s, bluebirds almost became extinct. But today, all three species—eastern, western (top right) and mountain (far right)—are at healthy population levels, and the future looks bright.

They still face challenges, however, such as competition for nesting sites from house sparrows, house wrens, European starlings and tree swallows. Often, just about the time a pair of bluebirds begins to nest, one of the four enemy birds takes over.

House wrens will even poke holes in the bluebirds' eggs. The frustrating part of this aggressive behavior is that once they win the battle, these other bird species often vacate the house.

Nesting starts early among bluebirds, so they can raise at least two broods each year. It's common for the young of the first brood to help their parents feed the second brood, a practice known as "cooperative breeding."

Tree cavities are natural nesting places, but bluebirds readily accept man-made nest boxes. They should be made of untreated wood, 4 by 4 inches to 5 by 5 inches square and 7 inches high, with a 1½-inch entrance hole about 6 inches above the floor.

A removable overhanging lid makes for easy observation and cleaning. The box should be ventilated at the top and include drainage holes in the floor. Paint or stain it a natural color, then place it on a post 5 to 10 feet above the ground at the edge of an open grassy field, facing away from the wind and sun. (For more guidelines about location of nesting boxes, visit the North American Bluebird Society's website at *nabluebirdsociety.org*.)

Then sit back and wait for the show to begin. As the song says, these birds are truly the "bluebird of happiness," bringing excitement, color and adventure to any backyard.

how do BIRDS learn their SONGS?

From regional dialects to mimicry, the world of birdsongs is fascinating.

BY KENN AND KIMBERLY KAUFMAN

The music of wild birds is among the most glorious gifts of nature. It inspires us not just to be bird-watchers, but to be bird listeners as well. When we listen closely, this music arouses our curiosity. It makes us ask questions.

Why do some kinds of birds always sound pretty much the same, while individuals of some other species sound recognizably different? Why do some birds sing the same song over and over, while others seem to show off with varied playlists? To better understand, let's take a look at the way birds learn their songs in the first place.

Yellow warbler

Songs vs. Calls

Most of our familiar backyard birds, from thrushes and jays to orioles and goldfinches, are classified as songbirds. But many of the sounds they make are not considered songs at all. In fact, the sounds you hear regularly are usually considered calls.

Think about songs for a minute so you can compare. Birdsongs tend to be more complex and melodious than calls. Typically, only the males sing during nesting season because they're trying to establish their territories and attract mates. By comparison, calls are usually short, simple sounds, and the birds use them all season.

Flocks of American robins, for example, make a wide variety of clucking, chirping or lisping calls at any time of year. But when a male robin perches in a treetop at dawn in spring and says *cheerup cheerily cheerio cheerup* for an hour, that's a song.

Scientists know about another fascinating difference between calls and songs. Among most of the true songbirds, the calls are instinctive, so the birds are born with the ability to make them. But the songs are learned. Before it can sing, the young bird must hear the songs of its own species during the first few months of its life.

If it were possible for an indigo bunting, for example, to grow up without ever hearing its own kind, it would make normal calls. But it would never develop the ability to sing its species' distinctive song.

Early Learning

Even in the learning of songs, though, instinct plays a part. The young bird has the natural ability to recognize the songs of its own kind. The heartbeat of a young song sparrow will actually speed up when it hears a male of its own species singing; it doesn't react this way when it hears another kind of sparrow.

So we could say that the bird has a built-in template for learning the right song. Still, it must hear the song while it's young. After the first few months of life, it's often too late.

A typical songbird goes through four stages. First there is the critical learning period, when it must hear the songs of its own kind. Then there is a silent period, often several months, during which those songs are simply stored in its memory.

Then the bird enters the subsong period, when it starts to experiment with soft, rambling versions of the song, much the way a human baby babbles. Finally, there's a period of a few weeks when the bird perfects its performance, putting the syllables and sounds together into a typical song for its species.

It's also important to note that some birds continue learning new songs all their lives. This is especially true for birds that mimic the songs of other species. While we were writing this article, a lively starling in the maple tree in front of our house was doing perfect imitations of bluebirds, kestrels, meadowlarks, flickers and a dozen other kinds of birds.

Mockingbirds are famed—and named— for their ability to mimic all kinds of birds, as well as doorbells, phone ringtones and many of the other new sounds they hear throughout their lives. Other mimic birds that can fool the ear include catbirds, parrots and lesser goldfinches.

Regional Lessons

Because a young bird tends to learn the songs of its immediate neighbors, the locals all might sound pretty much the same. But the same species can sound very different in another region, so birds, like humans, may have local dialects.

The song dialects of white-crowned sparrows have been studied for decades. In some places, such as parts of the Pacific Coast and the Canadian Rockies, the song patterns of white-crowned sparrows may change noticeably every few miles, and local bird enthusiasts may be able to tell exactly where they are just by listening to the sparrows!

Although a young songbird has an instinct for recognizing and learning the song of its own kind, this instinct is not infallible. Sometimes a bird will learn the song of the wrong species. We have occasionally run across this—for example, a prairie warbler that perfectly sang the song of a field sparrow.

Sometimes these seeming mistakes have a practical side. Where the ranges of black-capped chickadees and Carolina chickadees come together, a male may learn and use the songs of both species to drive all possible rivals out of his territory.

American robins will make a variety of calls year-round, but they sing mainly in spring.

Indigo buntings, like many songbirds, learn their songs from one another.

Eurasian tree sparrows look to their parents to learn their songs.

Nature's Symphony

Although most typical songbirds learn their songs, there are other kinds of birds for which all the sounds are based on pure instinct. Mourning doves, for example, instinctively know how to make their mournful cooing. Members of the flycatcher family, such as phoebes, wood-pewees and kingbirds, also know their songs by instinct, and will develop the right song even if they don't get to hear their own kind.

One of the best examples of this is the brown-headed cowbird. Female cowbirds lay their eggs in the nests of other birds, so the baby cowbird is always raised by other species. But it somehow knows that it's a cowbird, and regardless of what it hears as a nestling, when it grows up it will sound just the way it should!

Learning more about how birds tune up their vocal instruments can enrich our appreciation of nature's symphony. The next time you're out and about, listen to the birds for a few minutes and see what you can pick out and learn.

Mourning doves instinctively know their mournful coo.

Kenn loves the song of this Western bird, the varied thrush.

Mockingbirds can mimic all kinds of birds, as well as doorbells, phone ringtones and many other new sounds they hear.

Birds With the Best Songs

Which birds have the most beautiful songs? That's entirely a matter of opinion, of course, but here are some of our personal favorites.

KIMBERLY'S PICKS

VEERY THRUSH: A series of descending, harmonizing notes with an ethereal quality.

BARRED OWL: Resounding series of deep, rich notes: *Who cooks for you? Who cooks for you all?*

GREATER ROADRUNNER: The timeless cartoon taught us that the bird said Meep-meep! In reality, a roadrunner's song is a series of descending, slurred coos.

KENN'S PICKS

VARIED THRUSH: A long, humming whistle, simple but haunting, hanging in the air in cool Northwestern forests.

WINTER WREN: Rippling, bubbling, tinkling, trilling, and running on and on.

WHITE-THROATED SPARROW: Clear whistles of *Oh, sweet Kimberly, Kimberly, Kimberly!*

A male American goldfinch is stunning in his bright-yellow summer plumage. The return of its vivid hues is No. 2 on our countdown of top spring sights.

the best bird
moments
of spring

We count down our 8 favorites.
How do they compare with yours?

BY KEN KEFFER

Eastern phoebes are early spring migrants and fly in at No. 8.

With spring weather, dark-eyed juncos head north for moment No 7.

We all need little signs of hope.

When the wind chill dips and another bout of cold weather shows up in the forecast, we start wishing and dreaming of spring more than ever. For gardeners, crocuses and daffodils poking up through the snow offer hope. But what about the birders? What cues do we look forward to?

This was no easy task, but after chatting about it with some bird friends and quizzing *Birds & Blooms* readers online, I finally narrowed my list down to eight great bird moments. Now, I'm not declaring this a perfect list—after all, birding varies throughout the country. A sign of spring in my Wisconsin backyard doesn't necessarily happen in my grandma's Wyoming garden. But I think it's a pretty good start.

Follow my countdown of some of the most celebrated and anticipated bird moments of spring. Do you agree with my No. 1 pick?

no. 8 Phoebes perched on the edge of yards

Most flycatchers wait until a few more bugs are available for eating before returning from their winter ranges. However, phoebes are able to adapt their diets, so they're among the earliest of the spring migrants.

Watch for the tail bobs of phoebes near the edge of your yard. They will nest in close proximity to humans, so their return is like welcoming an old friend back from winter vacation. Phoebes can build a nest on nearly any ledge, but why not make it easier for them? Just as you'd do for a robin, place a nesting shelf platform under your eaves and invite them into your backyard.

no. 7 Dark-eyed juncos flying north

The first phoebe sighting of the year is easy to record. But marking the departure of a species can also be an important indicator. For some folks, the junco is the ultimate snowbird. So when the juncos leave, spring has arrived. (Remember, though, that for birders in the far north, the return of the juncos signals the return of their spring.)

Other species can also frequent your backyard during the winter months but move on to greener pastures as you welcome spring. Perhaps you were lucky enough to host a flock of redpolls or siskins this winter. Treasure those cold-weather visitors because these irruptive nomads will head back north, where traces of winter linger.

no. 6
The tap, tap, tap of woodpeckers

Spring is the season for attracting a mate, and this will translate to the drumming of woodpeckers. Most of us rejoice at the sound of strumming woodpeckers—as long as they aren't tapping on our downspouts. This is just one sign of mating season, though. Keep an eye out around your backyard and try to spot other rituals—a male bird feeding a lady friend, courtship dances, males fluffing up their feathers for females. These are all signs that new life is ahead.

To attract woodpeckers, use a larger nest box designed specifically for woodpeckers. You might add a few wood chips to the bottom of the box to make it look even more appealing. Another easy way to bring woodpeckers to your yard is by offering high-fat foods. Suet can be a year-round treat. Peanuts, both in and out of the shell, are also popular.

no. 5
Red-winged blackbirds singing

Optimists might mark spring with the arrival of red-winged blackbirds. These folks fully accept that there might be another snowstorm or two, but the sight of these early migrants raises hopes that winter will eventually thaw out the marshes and spring will return.

Male red-winged blackbirds start staking out territories in early March, and the females follow eventually. It's hard to miss the arrival of these blackbirds in spring. They perch high up on the tops of cattails and belt out raucous calls. If you want to see them, head to marshy areas, but be wary, or at least wear a hat. They have a reputation for being strong defenders of their territory.

A Carolina wren gathering supplies is our No. 3 moment.

no. 4
Hummingbirds and orioles sipping sugar water

You know spring is in the air when you hang the first batch of nectar for the season. I have to relearn the sugar water recipe every spring, so let me save you that step—it's four parts water to one part sugar, and that's for both hummingbirds and orioles.

As these birds march northward from their winter homes in Central America, many fly directly across the Gulf of Mexico. They reach the Gulf states in early March and hit their more northern breeding grounds by April. Like the blackbirds, males arrive a week or two before the females.

Aside from putting out sugar-water feeders, you can entice orioles with fresh oranges or grape jelly. As for hummingbirds, it can really help to have early blooms out in the garden. If you're ready for both species, you might be able to attract them right away. Then they'll stop to nest, and you'll see them all summer.

no. 3
Wrens gathering nesting material

Spring is nesting season for most birds, and when you see a wren carrying nesting material, it definitely makes winter feel like a distant memory.

Most wrens get an early start on nesting. They are prolific breeders, cranking out two or three broods of nestlings each spring and summer. Research indicates young male house wrens set up territories closer to established males, perhaps as a way to ensure they are nesting in suitable areas.

Don't wait for the return of the cavity nesters before checking your nest boxes to make sure they're ready to go for the season. Replace or repair any that were damaged over winter, and rehang predator guards early. You can even hang pieces of string, yarn and other materials in an old suet cage to help provide material for nests.

The No. 1 pick is a robin digging for worms.

no. 2 The molting of goldfinches

Perhaps the most celebrated of bird molts is the spring change of the American goldfinch. Although goldfinches don't migrate, it might seem that they disappear from the landscape during winter. The males turn from vibrant yellow to a drab olive green during colder months, becoming less conspicuous. While molting goes nearly unnoticed in many species, the first subtle hint of lemon yellow on the male goldfinch is a classic sign that spring is upon us.

To bring these beloved birds to your yard, offer thistle seed year-round. Once you get them established, you can put up one of those giant tube feeders that can attract 20-plus birds at a time. As a bonus, you don't have to worry about squirrels with this type of feeder or seed.

no. 1 Robins digging for worms

Though a few hardy robins can overwinter in some pretty harsh conditions, these birds are still the ultimate sign of spring for many people. Just imagine that first robin scampering across the backyard—you know sunny days are around the corner.

This doesn't necessarily mean robins were in the South and are just now migrating. After all, we've seen plenty of pictures of robins hanging out in the snow. It's more about the timing. April showers bring May flowers, but that's not all. The rain brings thawing and worms to the surface, and that's why you start to see them plucking up the plump morsels of nutrition.

If you want to be especially welcoming to robins in your backyard, you could offer mealworms as a special treat (any bluebirds dropping by will love 'em, too). Another hospitable option is to put up a nesting shelf, since robins don't use birdhouses.

As a child, Ken loved seeing the first western meadowlark of spring.

did you know?

Learn a few facts about orioles, some of spring's most gorgeous birds.

15 It usually takes females about a week to build a nest, but in bad weather, it can take as long as 15 days.

3 If you want to attract orioles to your backyard, try these three foods:
- Sugar water
- Oranges
- Grape jelly

1990s The Baltimore and Bullock's oriole were considered the same species until the 1990s, when genetic testing helped separate them.

5 Many fruit growers think of orioles as pests because, with their love of sweet treats, they can wipe out crops. Five fruits you'll often see them munching are raspberries, crabapples, grapes, mulberries and cherries.

7 Orioles average about 7 inches long, similar in size to red-winged blackbirds and a good 1 to 3 inches shorter than robins.

2 Adult males are much more brightly colored than females, but the males don't get their brilliant plumage until their second year.

9 As many as nine different types of orioles will show up in North America, but of those, only five are common: the Bullock's, Baltimore, hooded, orchard and Scott's.

4 Females are known for their skill at nest weaving. They weave a nest about 4 inches deep and 4 inches across, with a small opening at the top about 2 to 3 inches wide.

These facts are courtesy of our friends at Cornell Lab of Ornithology and their website *allaboutbirds.org*.

flying the
western skies

Discover why
these birds rule
the wide-open
spaces of the
American
West.

BY KEN KEFFER

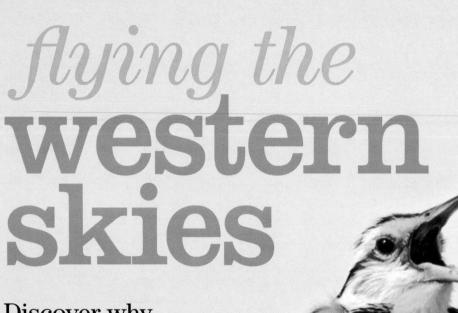

Six states have chosen
the western meadowlark
as their official state bird.

The Black Hills of western South Dakota are arguably the dividing line between Eastern and Western birds. I grew up about an hour west of there. Lately, I've lived to the far east of this avian divide, in places like Wisconsin, Ohio and Maryland, but I'll always be a Western boy at heart.

Birdlife is just different out west. Before I'd ever seen a blue jay or a northern cardinal, I'd seen their Western counterparts, the Steller's jay and the pyrrhuloxia. I know Eastern birds are more familiar to many readers, but let's take some time to explore some of these other noteworthy fliers.

Stars of the States

The western meadowlark is like the poster child for Western birds. It is the official bird of an impressive six states: Kansas, Montana, Nebraska, North Dakota, Oregon and Wyoming. The meadowlark proudly sings its cheery song from the tops of fence posts. For me, the sound always evokes memories of cattle ranches and wide-open spaces.

The lark bunting is the state bird of Colorado. White wing patches contrast with the black bodies of the males and the brown bodies of the females. More closely related to the sparrows than other buntings, the lark bunting is found throughout the Great Plains. And while many people think of Colorado as a mountain state, a summer visit to the eastern half of the state would offer you a good look at this dapper bird.

The plumage of mountain bluebirds is a near match for the vibrant hue of the Western sky. The state bird of Idaho lacks the rusty reds seen on eastern and western bluebirds. Mountain bluebirds prefer more open habitats than the other bluebird species. They are cavity nesters, though, and will readily use nest boxes. Mountain bluebirds range north to Alaska in the summer and can wander widely in the winter, occasionally showing up far to the east.

Another state bird is the California gull—though it represents Utah, not California. This species is held in high regard in Utah: It's credited with saving the crops of early Mormon settlers from vast outbreaks of grasshoppers. Today a statue of one of these beloved gulls stands tall in Salt Lake City.

Pyrrhuloxias are like the cardinals of the Southwest. These birds are very territorial during nesting season and will nest among cactus.

This male lark bunting helps tend a well-concealed nest. (Can you see the nestlings peeking out?)

Frequent Backyard Fliers

In addition to the most common and widespread feeder birds, such as chickadees, mourning doves and American goldfinches, the West hosts some backyard birds you don't find in other parts of the country.

While the Baltimore oriole is the state bird of Maryland and a backyard favorite throughout the East, Bullock's is the oriole of the intermountain west. These two birds were once considered to belong to a single species called the northern oriole, but in the 1990s they were split into two distinct species based on genetics research. Male Bullock's have less black on the head and more white on the wings than Baltimores do; females can be tricky to identify. Like other orioles, Bullock's will readily feed on sugar water, oranges and grape jelly.

While ruby-throated hummingbirds are common in the East, the similar broad-tailed, which also has a red throat, is frequently seen in the West. Fond of mountain meadow habitats, the broad-tailed hummingbird adapts to survive cool night temperatures. It can lower its heart rate and body temperature to go into an overnight torpor. Cooler air settles into mountain valleys, so males, unencumbered by nesting duties, will also move upslope to conserve energy.

Two other hummingbird species that are common in the intermountain west are the calliope and rufous. Migrating hummingbirds make quick backyard stops to refuel, so keep your sugar water up, or plant some native flowers for a backyard buffet.

Honorable Mention

Found from southern Saskatchewan and the Dakotas to the West Coast, the lazuli bunting is a true bunting of the West. While not as intensely blue as the indigo bunting, the male is a rich turquoise blue above. Lazuli buntings use shrubby habitats, and you can sometimes see them at feeders. The song of the lazuli bunting is a series of syllables pieced together, with young males sampling bits of the songs around them to create their own unique mating tune.

West of the Great Plains, black-headed grosbeaks replace the rose-breasted grosbeak. Stout birds with thick, heavy bills, they can make short order of a tray of black oil sunflower seeds. The female black-headed will sing in the spring, and males and females share nesting and brooding duties. This species winters in central Mexico, where it occasionally feeds on wintering butterflies. Monarchs are notoriously poisonous, but the grosbeaks can consume them sporadically with no ill effects.

Like the northern oriole, the rufous-sided towhee is a species that has been divided in two—in this case, into eastern and spotted towhees. Towhees live in shrubby areas

Mountain bluebirds will nest in cavities or nest boxes.

Bullock's oriole

Did you know there's no such thing as a seagull? Nope, they're just called gulls. This is the California gull, common in the West. It's the state bird of Utah.

The Steller's jay is loud, feisty and completely gorgeous. A western cousin of the blue jay, it will readily come to backyard feeders or picnic tables, hoping for a bite to eat.

Lazuli buntings have rusty chests like bluebirds.

and can be coaxed out of hedgerows by liberally sprinkling seed directly on the ground. They use a two-footed scratch as they feed.

One of my favorite birds was a towhee hybrid I spotted in Wyoming one fall, a cross between a spotted towhee and yet another Western towhee, the green-tailed. I made sure to feed it every evening right under its favorite lilac bush, and it lingered well into winter.

The West can be defined in any number of ways. For years, anything west of St. Louis was considered the frontier. I'd argue that there's plenty of land west of "out west." Folks on the West Coast might even have to go east to find some of these Western birds.

As a native, I'm biased, but I'd say Wyoming and the intermountain west are the heart of the West. And I like to think that these fascinating Western birds would agree.

BUNTING: DAVE WELLING; OWL: STEVE BYLAND

Burrowing owls differ from other owls—you must look down instead of up to find them. They're found throughout the West.

Western Birding
hot spots

The High Plains are as much a part of the Western landscape as mountain peaks. In these places, you might be rewarded with sightings of stunning birds like the McCown's longspur and the long-billed curlew.

COLORADO: Pawnee National Grasslands
The buttes and bluffs here are nesting places for several Western raptors, including Swainson's and ferruginous hawks, golden eagles and prairie falcons.

MONTANA: Charles M. Russell National Wildlife Refuge
Including prairies, badlands, forested coulees, river bottom and the vast Fort Peck Reservoir, this refuge encompasses over a million acres, running along the Missouri River for 125 miles as the crow flies.

NORTH DAKOTA: Little Missouri National Grassland/Teddy Roosevelt National Park
The classic western North Dakota landscape is on full display here. The area includes nearly 30,000 acres of wilderness, a rare designation for lands of the Great Plains.

SOUTH DAKOTA: Buffalo Gap National Grassland/Badlands National Park
Mixed grass prairie contrasts with the rugged badlands hills near Wall, South Dakota. In addition to diverse birds, this area is home to a reintroduced population of endangered black-footed ferrets.

WYOMING: Thunder Basin National Grassland
This patchwork of lands scattered throughout Wyoming's northeast corner is home to sage grouse and burrowing owls as well as prairie dogs and pronghorn.

birding
for your health

Discover why birds can do wonders for your physical and mental well-being.

BY KENN AND KIMBERLY KAUFMAN

You know the old saying "An apple a day keeps the doctor away"? Well, you could say that about birds. Sure, watching, photographing and feeding birds is a fun hobby, but there's much more to it than that. This simple activity can provide major health benefits and add to the quality of life for just about anyone.

We're always trying to persuade more people to take up an interest in birds, and now we have one of our best reasons yet. Go birding—it's good for you! Take a look at how a little dose of feathered friends and Mother Nature can have a big impact on your well-being.

FIND JOY. It's true that birds bring us happiness. Whether it's a female ruby-throat at a zinnia or a bluebird pair, they definitely give us something to look forward to day after day.

Let birds make you happy.

Although it's possible to do a lot of birding just by looking out the window, sooner or later birds will lure us outdoors. While this alone can lift your spirits, there really is a scientific tie between your mood and being outside.

When we're outdoors moving around and breathing fresh air, we tend to take deeper breaths. With more oxygen transported to all the cells of our bodies, including our brains, we become more alert, and our mood is likely to be elevated.

Also, during half an hour in the sun, we can soak up almost a whole day's requirement of vitamin D. Vitamin D is important for our physical health in a variety of ways, and it also helps to alleviate anxiety and depression.

Make new friends.

Studies have shown repeatedly that a strong network of friends will help you to stay happy and healthy. And if you take up bird-watching, you'll probably discover many new friendships. An interest in birds brings together people from all walks of life and of all ages and backgrounds. Birding crosses all social and economic barriers and creates a sense of camaraderie that can help forge lasting friendships.

Sharing our love of birds with new friends—and with those who have never tried birding—is beneficial for the birds, too! The more people we can get interested in birds and nature, the more support we build for conservation.

Head outdoors to get physical.

Birding can be as low-key and relaxing as sitting in a comfortable chair and watching the birds at your feeders. But it can also qualify as wonderful exercise. Simply going for a walk might be boring, but going for a walk to look for birds gives you a focus and a reason to keep going. And if you get serious about seeking new and different birds, you may find yourself hiking long distances and carrying all kinds of birding gear.

Even if you stay close to home, bird feeding also requires some physical activity. This is especially true if, like us, you live in an area where you have to shovel several inches of snow (or sometimes several feet!) from around your feeding station in winter. Use the birds in your backyard as inspiration to keep moving.

Go outside your comfort zone.

Pursuing birds in their natural habitats is bound to shake us out of our normal routines and haunts. Watching the sun rise over a meadow, going out into the woods at night to look for owls, even going to the landfill to see a rare gull—all of these take us beyond ordinary experiences.

For many birders, once they've gotten to know the birds in their area, there's an insatiable curiosity about species elsewhere in the world. Birding can be the motivation to travel far and wide. For instance, Kenn has watched birds on every continent. We're not suggesting that everyone should go to that extreme, but visiting new and different places and exploring the bird life there is an exciting way to expand your knowledge of the world at large.

HUMMINGBIRD: SARI ONEAL/SHUTTERSTOCK.COM; BLUEBIRDS: CAROL L. EDWARDS

Try something new.

Variety is the spice of life. This is an old saying, but it's true. Lack of variety in our lives can lead to boredom and a general sense of fatigue. Adding variety can make us more energized and positive, giving us more to look forward to. And of course, in terms of variety, birds offer a dizzying array of colors, calls and behaviors.

You can't predict all the birds you'll see while going out birding. On any given day, some of the expected birds will be nowhere to be seen while totally unexpected ones may pop up at any moment. So birding offers both a reassuring sense of the predictable and an exciting sense of the unpredictable, keeping us on our toes and alive to the possibilities.

Get in touch with Mother Nature.

An interest in birds can be the gateway to an even wider world of discovery. Once you go outdoors and start looking around, it's almost impossible to just see the birds. Before long, a beautiful butterfly, an intriguing mushroom or some unfamiliar turtle will distract you. It's OK to be distracted—the birds won't mind.

As we're fond of saying, when you learn more about nature, your view of the world becomes more three-dimensional. Some of our best friends are humans, but there are about a million other species of living things out there that are also worth knowing.

Feed the birds to feed your brain.

Keeping our minds active and healthy is essential for our overall sense of well-being. The Alzheimer's Association suggests that if we want to keep our brains healthy we need to keep learning new things. What better way to do that than by continuing to learn about birds? If you are new to bird-watching, just identifying the birds you see can be a challenging mental puzzle. If you are an experienced birder, you can still learn new things every day about the behavior of your local birds.

Studies have shown that these kinds of mental exercises can help form new neural paths that can help fight back against diseases like Alzheimer's, other forms of dementia and Parkinson's. So find a little time to put out a feeder and watch to see what shows up. After all—it's good for you.

Thanks to the Birds

Readers share stories about how birding has made a difference for their physical, mental and emotional health.

A few years ago, I was diagnosed with Rocky Mountain spotted fever. It affected my health in many ways, including the circulation in my legs. I couldn't stand longer than 30 minutes at a time, so I started watching and photographing the birds on my patio to keep myself occupied. This pastime became my therapy. The birds have helped me get through some very tough times, and they give me something to look forward to each day. Just recently, I was officially diagnosed as being disabled. I know it's going to be challenging, but I'm glad I can still enjoy one of my favorite passions in life—birds!
Tom King ELIZABETHTOWN, KENTUCKY

One summer I found myself hyperventilating on my laundry room floor from a panic attack (although I didn't know that at the time). For the following week the attacks were constant; I couldn't eat, I couldn't sleep, and every time my husband left for work I was terrified of being alone with my 1- and 3-year-old children. I spent the time he was gone pacing the house, unable to stop moving for fear of giving my mind a chance to panic again. On day six, as I left the doctor's feeling defeated once again, a very urgent thought popped in my head: I needed a hummingbird feeder!

A few mornings later I was up early when I heard the telltale buzzing of a little hummingbird flitting around. Throughout that day I would stop everything I was doing to watch her. I realized that during those moments, that gut-wrenching anxious feeling was gone for just a few seconds. It was then I realized that I wasn't going to succumb to this feeling of panic; I had hope again! As time went by, the panic attacks lessened, and I was able to enjoy time with my family again. As it turns out, that hummingbird opened up some amazing new experiences for me!

Emily Woodmansee
FORT DRUM, NEW YORK

I'm a 27-year-old ballet and hip-hop dancer. Dancing is my world, but a couple of years back I had a knee injury that I've never fully recovered from. I now realize there will come a day when I can no longer dance, and this crushes me. However, I've also learned that there are other things in life—like birds. During the past couple of years, I discovered I love birding almost as much as I love dance. My friends make fun of me a bit, but I'm just so happy to have this passion in my life! No matter how old I get, birding will always be with me. This has given me a lot of hope and has completely changed my life in a positive way.

Katie Long IOWA CITY, IOWA

In 2005 and 2006, I suffered two deep losses that shook me to my core—first my mother and then my husband. I probably should have fallen apart, but instead I filled up my bird feeders and started learning photography. My friends and family have been so supportive, and their encouragement feeds the flame of my addiction to Mother Nature.

Carol Estes LAPORTE, INDIANA

GO EXPLORING. You'll always find inspiring birds when you venture outside of your own backyard. Perhaps you'll see a Wilson's warbler (here) or eastern screech-owls (above).

FEED THE BIRDS.
Whether you plant berries for waxwings or put out peanuts for the red-bellied woodpeckers, it's very gratifying to feed the birds.

On an entirely physical level, birding has changed the very way I walk. Before I started birding, I used to walk with my head down, charging at a fast pace. When I walked with my spouse, I sped ahead much faster than her. After any distance, I would end up on my own, and she would be far behind me. "Why do you walk so slow?" I used to ask. Now, because of birding, I walk with her at almost a snail's pace, looking and appreciating so much more in nature than I ever saw before.
Deb Neidert KENT, OHIO

I've always enjoyed watching birds and wildlife, even as a young child. But then, in 1995, I was diagnosed with a painful chronic illness that pretty much confined me to my one-bedroom apartment. My mom suggested I get a bird feeder to hang in the tree outside my living room. After that, I spent many days sitting on my couch and watching the different kinds of birds come to feed. Eventually I got a bird book and binoculars and was able to identify the birds that showed up, as well as their songs. Now, 17 years later, I still start my day by looking out the window to see who is at the feeder and listening for their sweet morning songs.
Diane Hollister
NASHVILLE, TENNESSEE

a new appreciation for sparrows

Learn why you shouldn't overlook this charming family of birds.

BY SALLY ROTH

Chipping sparrow

It's easy to lump all sparrows together: "Yep, looks like a sparrow to me."

You can find at least 33 species of native sparrows across the U.S. And while their plumage won't sweep you off your feet the way an oriole's or a bluebird's will, they're still worth your time and attention.

Fall and winter bird feeding just wouldn't be the same without these little brown birds. They liven up the feeder scene as they hop about, pecking in the tray, scratching for seeds beneath the feeder or gleaning the garden for leftover seeds.

Another of their charming traits: All sparrows are singers. Their styles vary from the achingly sweet song of the fox sparrow to the unexpected buzz of the grasshopper sparrow to the melancholy phrases of the white-throated. But almost all are a delight to listen to.

And once you take a closer look, you'll see that sparrows have a beauty all their own. Check out your feeder birds with binoculars, starting with the head, both to appreciate their subtle allure and to figure out who's who.

Our Winter Friends

These native sparrows are beloved feeder friends from fall through spring in most parts of the country; then they take off for summer breeding grounds to the north. Luckily for us, the birds begin singing before they leave our feeders in late spring.

White-throated sparrow

WHITE-THROATED SPARROW.
Abundant and familiar, the white-throat is easy to identify by its snowy bib. Until I spent some time in New England, I couldn't figure out why people spell out the song *Old Sam Peabody-Peabody-Peabody.* Turns out the name is pronounced "Peabiddy" there—just as the sparrow says.

WHITE-CROWNED SPARROW.
This dashing bird is an eye-catcher, its head topped with bold white stripes. This species leaves us about the time dandelions are turning to puffs: The parachute-topped seeds are a favorite food. Next time you see a white-crowned sparrow, consider the journey it's about to embark on, which may take it to nesting grounds above the Arctic Circle. Time for an extra helping!

Fox sparrow

Song sparrow

FOX SPARROW. Even a brief visit from a fox sparrow—and that's all we get in most places—is an occasion. They're big, bold and a beautiful chestnut color (at least in the eastern U.S.) and, boy, can they sing! In the West, their color is much duller, leaning toward gray in the Rockies and most of California, and brown along the coast.

The Backyard Nesters

Many sparrow species may visit a feeder, especially during migration, but only a few are willing to call our backyards home. The sage sparrow, swamp sparrow, seaside sparrow and many others have specialized habits that require more than the typical yard can offer.

SONG SPARROW. The most widespread sparrow, this year-round species begins singing in late winter, a welcome herald of spring. It often nests in backyards, tucking its cup of grasses right on the ground in your flower bed or strawberry patch. Song sparrows vary so much in coloring across their range that you may think you're seeing several different species. Once they open their mouths, though, they all sound the same.

CHIPPING SPARROW. The monotone trill of the tiny chippy is easy to overlook in the spring chorus of birdsong. A resident during nesting season across most of the country, this little chipping bird often hides its home in backyard shrubs. Watch for the cute little rusty-capped chippy hopping about on the ground to collect stray hairs from your dog to line its delicate nest.

The Sparrows Afield

Many native sparrows refuel at our feeders during migration, but not all become regulars. Keep an eye out for these little brown birds of the field when you're hiking or driving. Depending on where you live, these widespread birds may be summer nesters or winter residents, or you may see them only during migration.

VESPER SPARROW. This bird looks like a bigger song sparrow until its white outer tail feathers give it away. Its lovely music, too, resembles the song sparrow's: a few whistles to start, followed by a quickening trill. Naturalist and essayist John Burroughs named the bird after the sweet, peaceful music of a sunset church service.

SAVANNAH SPARROW. Grasslands across the country—also known as savannas or savannahs—are where you'll find this bird. It's the quintessential sparrow: a small, streaky-breasted brown bird that lies low until it's time to sing. Then, look for the savannah holding forth from a fence post, road sign or tree.

GRASSHOPPER SPARROW. You'll hear this small, shy sparrow way more often than you'll set eyes on it. Why grasshopper? Two reasons: It lives in fields and pastures, and it makes a sibilant buzz very much like an insect's. Like other grassland birds, its numbers are declining sharply, so look and listen while you can.

White-crowned sparrow

Grasshopper sparrow

Vesper sparrow

Savannah
sparrow

A Whole
New World

You've no doubt noticed
one familiar sparrow
missing from these
pages—the house or
English sparrow. That
one is an Old World
transplant, unrelated to
our native New World
species. You can find
out more about sparrows
of both worlds, as well
as other birds, in Sally
Roth's new book, *An
Eye on the Sparrow*,
available at *sallyroth.com*
and other sites. It takes
a look at the natural
behavior behind every
Bible verse about birds—
how the science behind
the Scriptures helps us
understand those verses
even more.

bird tales

Readers share some of their best birding stories.

Double Delight

We've fed orioles for the past several years, and are lucky enough to have both Bullock's and hooded species visit us. Last year they arrived late, and we became concerned they wouldn't show up at all. But as summer set in, adults and young flocked to our feeders. Here's one female Bullock's that gives the impression she would like to see the feeder a little less crowded!

Ray Nelson PAGE, ARIZONA

Top That

Rescuing a goldfinch that hit our large window, I picked it up in a towel and walked over to show my husband. The finch soon got its bearings and decided to fly up onto my husband's head! It rested there for about 10 minutes, giving me time to fetch my camera. I told our friends that I finally have proof my husband is a birdbrain.

Barbara Scheller MURPHY, NORTH CAROLINA

Fly, Finch, Fly!

Last spring, a little American goldfinch flew into our front window and startled itself. Another goldfinch stood beside it on our deck. My daughter, Abby, picked them both up and moved them to the picnic table to get them away from our dogs. The one on her finger—the one that hit the window—wouldn't let go. Eventually its friend flew off. Abby worried that the other one was too injured to fly. She gave it some direction, holding her arms out and saying, "You just spread your wings and fly!" The bird must've listened, as it immediately flew away!

Melissa Holland CALVERT CITY, KENTUCKY

A Prefab Home!

While reading in my flower garden, I felt a tugging at my curly ponytail, which I had pulled atop my head that day instead of leaving it at the back, as usual. Engrossed in my book, I didn't really think much about it. I kept reading, but the tugging returned, slightly more insistent. So I put down my book and soon identified the persistent pest: a robin. Apparently a female, building her nest, saw my nestlike hairdo and thought she'd hit the jackpot. Laughing, I yelled out, "Hey! That's my bird nest, not yours!"

Suzette Wilkins ALANSON, MICHIGAN

Wonderful Waders

I was so excited when I spotted these American avocets wading near the shore of nearby Winona Lake last spring. Having never seen this species before, I was determined to get photos. I sat for a long time, letting the watchful avocets get used to me; then I moved closer and waited again. It took some time, but even one good photo of a new water bird makes all the effort worthwhile!

Ted Rose NORTH MANCHESTER, INDIANA

Walking With Stilts

In August 2011, I spent a few weeks on the Hawaiian island of Kauai, with paradise as my backyard. While I was doing some early-morning photography in the taro fields, this black-necked stilt posed prettily next to some orange blossoms and opened its bill. What a wonderful opportunity!

Becca Nelson LINCOLNSHIRE, ILLINOIS

Building a Home Together

Early last March, my wife and I visited Everglades National Park. We saw many species of birds up close, but the most special treat was finding this pair of anhinga during a nest-building ritual. The male (left) made frequent trips for building materials while the female constructed the nest. In this snapshot they're working together to position a twig.

Dean Rushmore MARYSVILLE, OHIO

Brainy Bird

This downy woodpecker must have grown tired of carrying seeds into trees to crack them and eat the kernels. It dug a hole in a dead limb next to the feeder, where, with little effort, it could grab a seed, trap it and hammer out the innards. Smart little bird.

Norman Cline
MOUNT CARMEL, ILLINOIS

Holiday Hoo-ligan!

At Christmastime, my husband looked out our kitchen window and noticed something in our holiday wreath. This eastern screech-owl appears to have slept while Ron took its picture. What a wonderful holiday surprise!

Diana Bridge HAMILTON, OHIO

OSPREYS REALLY KNOW HOW TO FISH. They've even earned the nickname "fish hawk."

amazing and rare RAPTORS

Find out why these uncommon birds of prey are some of the most captivating in the bird world.

BY KEN KEFFER

Gyrfalcons are the largest falcons in the world. They spend most of their time in the northernmost parts of North America.

Northern hawk owls are a mostly northern species and have long, hawklike tails.

Mississippi kites summer in the Great Plains and feast on insects.

Some consider raptors the bad boys (and girls) of the bird world, but I think it's unfortunate that they've acquired that reputation. Sure, their antics may seem gruesome, but they are among nature's finest hunters. And yes, it seems that almost everyone has a tale of a Cooper's hawk harassing backyard birds. But if you can forgive raptors for thinking of your songbirds as a buffet, they really are some of the most fascinating birds you'll ever see.

Many raptors are widespread and common, such as red-tailed hawks and the northern saw-whet owl, but let's explore some of the lesser-known avian carnivores.

A Raptor Refresher

Lumped together not by taxonomy but by behavior, raptors make a living eating other critters. Also known as birds of prey, this group includes hawks, eagles, owls, falcons, harriers, kites and ospreys. Some people include New World vultures and condors, too, but these species are really more like scavengers than true hunters.

Predatory birds share similar characteristics and adaptations, including sharp beaks and talons and strong feet. Interestingly, most raptors use their feet for harvesting their prey, while the beak's function is to tear off meat. To varying degrees, female raptors are often larger than their male counterparts; this allows the sexes to feed on different items of prey.

Some raptors are generalists and will eat a wide range of food that may include small mammals, birds, reptiles, amphibians, insects and carrion. But other raptors are very particular. Birds dominate the diet of accipiters, like the familiar Cooper's and sharp-shinned hawks. On the other hand, many of the soaring hawks and the larger owls are specialized small-mammal predators. Smaller raptors tend to consume a larger percentage of insects.

Graceful Flying Kites

Hawks, owls and even eagles are fairly widespread, but kites are a group of birds that have a somewhat limited range in the U.S., where they're mostly confined to the Southeast and the West Coast.

These medium-size raptors are also some of the most buoyant and graceful fliers. Their diet ranges from rodents to terrestrial snails, with insects making up a large portion of the intake of many kite species.

The most widespread among this group is the Mississippi kite. Long a common bird in the southern Great Plains and the Southeast, this species has recently been establishing new nesting areas.

Landscape changes to the north have created more kite-friendly habitats, and Mississippi kites now nest in Colorado, New Hampshire, Ohio and points in between. These birds will often catch insects on the wing and then consume them in flight.

The swallow-tailed kite is a striking white bird with black edging along the wings and a long, black, deeply forked tail. This kite is limited in range to the Gulf Coast and north along the Eastern Seaboard to South Carolina. Familiar on the West Coast, the white-tailed kite can also be found along the southern tier from Arizona to Florida. White-tailed kites can be spotted hovering in flight before pouncing upon an unsuspecting rodent.

Seeing a kite is always exciting. I have not encountered many, so to me they're the most exotic of the raptors.

South by Southwest Specialties

Like kites, a number of hawks are common in Mexico and areas south but have a limited range north of the border. You'll need to visit the American Southwest to spot common black-hawks and gray, white-tailed, short-tailed and zone-tailed hawks.

One species that's a bit more widespread in the border region is the Harris's hawk, found in the desert and brush country from Arizona to south Texas. The Harris's hawk exhibits a rare raptor behavior called communal hunting. This species will remain together as a family unit, so the group can cooperatively hunt prey as large as jackrabbits.

Another Southwestern species to look for is one of the smallest birds of prey—the elf owl. Found mostly in Arizona, this raptor is about the size of a sparrow. Don't let those adorable oversize eyes fool you, though. Elf owls are efficient insect predators.

One other raptor worth mentioning is the Aplomado falcon. It was wiped out in the U.S. by the 1950s, but efforts to restore it to the Southwest have started to pay off. Like other falcons, this one feeds mostly on birds. This vibrant species has begun to appear in the southern shrublands of Texas and New Mexico.

Hunters of the Far North

Some raptors eke out a living at the far northern edge of the continent, far away from most of us. Birds like the great gray owl, northern hawk owl, gyrfalcon and northern goshawk rarely venture south, except when extreme cold forces them to seek food elsewhere.

Another species to look for is the rough-legged hawk, a regular winter migrant throughout the U.S. You'll find these small-mammal specialists in open farmlands and prairies. Their dark bellies and large black patches on the underwing make them easy to pick out, even in flight. On long winter drives, rough-legged hawks can be the only signs of life at times.

The winter habits of snowy owls are much less regular. They don't have a classic migration pattern but instead make irruptive movements south to the northern U.S. in search of food. Snowy owls like to perch atop schools or other buildings, so keep an eye out for them.

Truly a collection of unique and intriguing birds, raptors have an unmatched grace and subtle beauty. They deserve respect, too: From the widespread American kestrel to the localized ferruginous pygmy-owl, being a bird of prey is a tough life.

Swallow-tailed kites are mostly concentrated in Florida and are known for their forked tails.

the best in bird-watching

Harris's hawks gather in groups to hunt together.

GO SEE RAPTORS
Located in southwestern Idaho, the Snake River Birds of Prey National Conservation Area protects critical raptor nesting habitat along an 81-mile stretch of the Snake River Canyon. This unique environment supports the highest density of raptor nests in North America, with more than 700 nests located here. Throughout the year, more than 20 raptor species can be found at this hot spot. Nesting species include prairie and peregrine falcons, American kestrels, golden eagles, red-tailed and ferruginous hawks, northern harriers and ospreys. Seven species of owls also nest here: the great horned, burrowing, long-eared, short-eared, northern saw-whet, barred and western screech-owl.

did you know?

1
There's one easy way to find a northern harrier—go for a drive in the country. You'll see these birds swooping and soaring over open fields.

80
Bald eagles (here) and golden eagles have wingspans of about 80 inches, among the largest of all birds of prey.

6,000
Swainson's hawks are common in the American West, where they gather in flocks and migrate more than 6,000 miles to wintering grounds in South America. But a few get off the track and fly to Florida in the winter.

3 Only three North American hawks have feathered legs all the way to their toes.
1. Rough-legged hawk
2. Ferruginous hawk
3. Golden eagle (above)

2 The snowy owl and barn owl are the only two large, light-colored owls in North America. But the similarities stop there. In fact, snowy owls are rarely spotted south of the Canadian border.

glad you asked!

Birding expert George Harrison answers your questions.

A male American robin, singing in a flowering red maple

◀ It seems that one bird starts singing each morning and then other birds join in. How is the leader bird chosen?

Carol Phiambolis

BLUE BELL, PENNSYLVANIA

GEORGE: The dawn chorus you refer to is best in spring, when all the breeding birds are present. In my experience, the American robin starts it off. If other native thrushes are in the mix—yes, the robin is a thrush— then one of those might beat the robin to it. A more complete answer depends on where you live and the natural habitat around your home. But you're right: They do all seem to join in right after the first soloist.

▲ Last July 21, I heard a cardinal singing and noticed a pair coming and going from a nest with twigs. Is it unusual for cardinals to nest in July?

Connie Garland GREENWOOD, INDIANA

GEORGE: A pair of cardinals will typically try to have two or three broods of young in different nests each summer. (Four is possible but rare.) If a predator or the weather destroys a nest, the pair may replace it later in the summer. It's likely that the pair you saw in late July had at least attempted to nest once or twice before in a different location.

We regularly see downy and red-bellied woodpeckers at our feeders, but never have any nuthatches. We offer peanuts, suet, seeds and more. How can we attract nuthatches?
Kim Luzum LEAWOOD, KANSAS

GEORGE: Nuthatches are exclusively tree-trunk birds. If you don't have trees—especially big ones with substantial trunks—around your feeders, these birds may not be comfortable in your yard. Nuthatches shuffle down tree trunks headfirst to find insects that are hidden from woodpeckers, which scoot up those same trunks. They're especially fond of black-hulled sunflower seeds in the shell. Try offering only sunflower seeds to see if you can coax them to your feeders.

▼ At first I thought this bird was a dove, but when I saw it move its head in a circle I realized it was an owl! What kind is it?
Patricia Austin PORT HOPE, ONTARIO

GEORGE: This is a northern saw-whet owl. Among the smallest owls in North America, saw-whets reside in southern Canada, the Great Lakes region, and the Northwest as far up as Alaska. This tiny owl lacks the "ear" tufts that some larger owls have.

Do birds put on extra feathers in cold weather?
Wanda Salsman LAKEWOOD, COLORADO

GEORGE: Yes, birds that must survive the cold will grow double their usual number of feathers to insulate their bodies. They also may look fatter because they fluff those feathers to create a thicker barrier against the elements. Birds will also shiver, snuggle and seek shelter inside birdhouses or tree cavities.

Sparrows inhabit my martin house all year. When should I clean, repair and paint it?
Roger Fink LOUISVILLE, OHIO

GEORGE: The best time to do the maintenance work on your martin house is in the fall or winter, when the martins are in Peru. Don't worry about destroying the sparrow nests. You likely have house sparrows, which are nonnatives and are not protected by law. Also, in winter, they're only roosting, not nesting.

I grew up near a 37-foot waterfall that was home to phoebes. How can I attract these birds to my backyard?
Roxanne Mustizer
SACKETS HARBOR, NEW YORK

GEORGE: Phoebes in the East and Midwest love water. All the phoebe nests I've ever seen were under the eaves of a lake cottage, at the entrance to a wet cave or under a bridge. Because they also like to nest on a shelf, I suggest that you place one where you want them to nest. If you're

Painted buntings often visit backyard feeders in the coastal southeast and south-central U.S.

anywhere near water, you might get lucky and attract these birds to your backyard.

▲ I've always wondered why I get multiple female painted buntings at my feeders but never see a male.
Pamela Johnson MELBOURNE, FLORIDA

GEORGE: Though there should be colorful males among the green females, one possible answer is that you have some first-year males that are still in green plumage. I have a number of friends living in Florida, including Melbourne Beach, who see painted buntings in winter, including adult males. So keep looking for them!

FAQ "Should I put out a birdbath in winter?"

GEORGE: Birds are well-equipped to find drinking water in winter, but adding a bath will definitely get you some backyard traffic. If you want to provide water, put out a heated birdbath. When the temperatures are below freezing, birds will drink the water but are unlikely to bathe in it.

Northern cardinal
Photo by Jeff Turek

Northern saw-whet owl
Finalist in our Backyard Photo Contest
Photo by Sandra Seehafer-Dziok

Great crested flycatcher
Finalist in our Backyard Photo Contest
Photo by Dale Matuza

American goldfinch
Finalist in our Backyard Photo Contest
Photo by Jean Bullock

Ruby-throated hummingbird
Winner in our Backyard Photo Contest
Photo by Lance Bruce

CHAPTER 2

Hummingbird *heaven*

Find endless enjoyment in the antics of the liveliest little fliers. Read about quick and easy ways to increase the hummingbird traffic in your yard. Plant the shrubs and flowers that are sure to lure these miniature friends.

CAROL L. EDWARDS

Ruby-throated
hummingbird

think like a
hummingbird

Our birding experts get inside their heads and come up with some indispensable advice for enticing them.

BY KENN AND KIMBERLY KAUFMAN

Hummingbirds are some of the most fascinating and flashy fliers you'll ever see. Yet they're also some of the most misunderstood.

If you want to attract them and keep them coming around (and don't we all?), you might not be sure how to get started. After all, a lot of information is out there, and it's a little overwhelming trying to decide what to believe or try.

To provide a little insight into these tiny feathered gems, we thought we would get inside their heads a bit and think the way they do. Of course, we can't really think like hummingbirds. But we have studied their behavior enough over the years to make some good guesses about what they're thinking. Here's what they might advise if they could.

"Use red! It really does work."

In North America, the flowers best adapted for hummingbird pollination are bright red blooms with a tubular shape. Hummers instinctively watch for red things and investigate them. (We've seen them making detours to check out the taillights of parked cars, and even someone's sunburned nose!) There's no question that planting red flowers will help bring hummingbirds to your yard.

DID YOU KNOW? This hummingbird is feeding on crocosmia, which is actually a bulb.

"We don't need fancy food."

Some companies sell hummingbird nectar, but you can easily make your own. Measure out 1 part white sugar to 4 parts water and mix thoroughly. If you boil the mixture to remove impurities, it may keep longer before it starts to spoil. Don't mix in any honey, red dye or other additives.

"Keep it clean."

Sugar water that has started to grow moldy can be dangerous to birds. If you're going to put out feeders, it's essential that you keep them clean and replace the mixture regularly—at least once every three or four days, more often in hot weather. If the mixture starts to look cloudy, clean the feeder and replace the nectar immediately.

DID YOU KNOW?
Juvenile male and female ruby-throats look similar. Males will usually get their full red gorgets during their first winter.

A black-chinned and rufous hummingbird share space at this sugar-water feeder.

"Put it out in the open."

Hummers are always looking around for food sources, and they're good at finding them, but you can help by putting your feeder in a place where it's easy to spot. Use a feeder with some bright red on it, and position it where it can be seen by birds flying past at a distance.

"Give us some space."

Goldfinches and some other songbirds may feed together peacefully, but hummingbirds often fight around feeders, chasing one another away. Hummers are adapted to feeding at flowers, which will produce only limited amounts of nectar, so they instinctively protect their food sources even when they're at feeders with an unlimited supply. Try putting up two or more feeders that can't be seen from one another. Even the toughest little hummer can't monopolize multiple feeders if he or she can't see them all at once.

"We're creatures of habit."

If the hummingbirds returning in spring seem to remember where you had flowers or feeders in previous years, they probably do. As tiny creatures that rely on specialized food sources in a big, big world, they have to be good at finding their way back to the best spots. They have a highly developed sense of what scientists call spatial memory. This is a good reason to work extra hard at attracting them. Once you get them established, they'll be back for more.

"It's not you. It's me."

While the hummingbirds enjoy having your backyard as a nectar source, they aren't relying on you 100 percent. One of the top questions we are asked is: "If I have my feeder out in fall, will it keep the hummers from migrating?" The answer is no. They'll migrate when they're ready, whether or not feeders are available. It's instinct!

"Leave it to the ladies."

Backyard birders sometimes worry because they had a pair of hummingbirds around and then the male disappeared, leaving a single mother behind. But this is normal for hummers. The male never helps with nest building, incubation or feeding the young. The amazing mother hummingbird does all that work herself. Meanwhile, the male goes off in search of another female. It seems odd to humans, but this behavior ensures that there will be even more hummingbirds for us to enjoy!

"Stay alert, but be patient."

It may take some time for hummers to find your feeder—and even after they do, it may be awhile before you notice that they're visiting. They may zip in to the feeder for a quick sip many times before you happen to catch them in the act. So keep the feeder ready, and keep watching. You're likely to be richly rewarded.

DID YOU KNOW? Hummingbird nests (near left) are about the size of a pingpong ball. Anna's hummingbirds (top left) are common all along the West Coast. If you look closely, you might see their tiny nests (far left) perched on branches of shrubs and trees.

DID YOU KNOW?
The magnificent hummingbird was known as Rivoli's hummingbird until the name changed in the 1980s.

say hello to hummingbirds

Follow the chart for quick solutions to attract and feed hummingbirds.

Want to attract more hummingbirds?

Do you have...

A large garden

LUCKY!
You can go crazy with plants and bushes hummingbirds love—cannas, fuchsia, pentas, hibiscus, salvia and columbine, to name just a few. Plant them all together for a real hummingbird haven.

A small space

DON'T WORRY.
Hummingbirds visit patios and balconies, too, with the right mix of plants. Try phlox, verbena, calibrachoa and petunias, which are all easy-care container plants.

One feeder

NO PROBLEM.
Since it's the only feeder you've got, make it count. Keep a close eye on it to make sure it's never empty, or the hummingbirds will lose interest. For a little extra impact, hang a basket of red impatiens nearby.

Several feeders

KEEP 'EM HAPPY.
To encourage several hummingbirds to visit regularly, space feeders out of sight of each other to prevent territorial competition. Try providing perches or even a misting water feature. Watching them fly through the mist is entertainment, too.

I've got hummingbirds, but I need some solutions to these feeder problems.

Ants or bees have taken over my feeder.

LET'S TAKE CARE OF IT.
For bees, make sure your feeder is equipped with bee guards. The best defense against ants is an ant moat, which is essentially just a cup of water hanging above your feeder to keep the ants from reaching the feeding port.

The sugar water goes bad so quickly.

DON'T LET IT SPOIL.
If possible, hang your feeder in the shade. And remember, it's crucial to keep the feeder clean and the sugar water fresh. (Don't forget, the recipe is 4 parts water to 1 part sugar.) If the sugar water is cloudy, it's time to replace it.

My feeder is so hard to clean.

YOU'RE NOT ALONE!
Some readers swear that an old toothbrush or bottle brush will reach all the crevices of a hummingbird feeder. Or try mixing a tablespoon of uncooked rice and water in the feeder and shaking vigorously. Rinse the feeders well after any cleaning.

top
10
blooming shrubs
of summer

*Offer hummingbirds and butterflies
a robust nectar source with shrubs
that boast summer flowers.*

BY STACY TORNIO

1

Gorgeous springtime blossoms…fantastic fall color…tasty winter berries: When it comes to shrubs, these seasonal delights come to mind first. But superb summertime blooms? Yes, actually! You can find a whole slew of shrubs that flower in summer, which makes them outstanding nectar sources for hungry little hummingbirds. So we couldn't think of a more fitting chapter than this one for our list of top 10 summer-blooming shrubs.

Add a couple of these to your backyard, and you'll keep the hummingbirds (and butterflies, like the fritillary on p. 66) happy for years to come.

1 Butterfly bush

Buddleja davidii, Zones 5 to 9

With arching spikes full of purple, white, pink or yellow florets, butterfly bush will bloom from midsummer through the first frost. Gardeners prize it for its impact—it can grow up to 15 feet, with hundreds of blossoms—and because it will endure drought and heat. Plant in full sun. Note that it's considered invasive in some areas, though new varieties are seedless; check before planting.

FAVORITES: The new choices are many, including several smaller varieties. Look for the Lo & Behold Blue Chip cultivar, which grows to only a couple of feet, or the English Butterfly Peacock, which tops out at about 5 feet.

2 Mockorange

Philadelphus, Zones 3 to 8

Once you see mockorange, you've got to have it. In early summer, the shrubs bear gorgeous pure white flowers that last for weeks and smell delicious. Most grow up to 6 feet tall, but you can also find compact or dwarf varieties. Grow in full sun.

FAVORITES: Look for Snow White Sensation, with its resplendent double blooms. It will flower in late spring or early summer and then will bloom again later in the season.

3 Spirea

Spiraea, Zones 3 to 8

If you want an easy-to-grow shrub with exciting color, look for a spirea at the garden center. While they provide several seasons of interest, it's the summer blooms that are most impressive. Sure, the individual flowers are tiny, but together they pack quite a punch. Spirea prefers full sun. It's important to find a cultivar that's right for your space—some grow only 18 inches tall, while others can get to be several feet.

FAVORITES: Many spirea blooms are white, so we like the cultivars that offer pink flowers as an alternative. Pink Parasols and Double Play are some of our favorites.

1: CAROL L. EDWARDS; 2,4: BAILEY NURSERIES; 3: PROVEN WINNERS

4 Potentilla

Potentilla fruticosa, Zones 2 to 7

It's one of the longest-blooming shrubs around, beginning to flower in late spring and then continuing until fall. Northern gardeners love it because it does well even in frigid Zone 2. Potentilla loves full sun and well-drained soil; blooms are typically yellow. The shrub is on the small side, from 1 to 4 feet tall, usually with a mounding habit.

FAVORITES: Coronation Triumph is one of the earliest-blooming potentillas. We also like Abbotswood, an introduction from the Netherlands that has few problems with insects or disease.

5 Bluebeard

Caryopteris, Zones 5 to 9

If you long for blue flowers, this bold little shrub could provide exactly what you're looking for. Most grow to only 2 or 3 feet high in full sun, making them a natural choice for limited space. The deep blue flowers emerge in late summer and keep right on blooming through fall. This one's a favorite of butterflies, too.

FAVORITES: We're partial to the Petit Blue cultivar because of its dramatic, compact growth and rich green foliage. We also like Blue Mist, known for its long bloom season and silvery-green leaves.

6 Viburnum

Viburnum, Zones 2 to 9

Among the most popular of ornamental shrubs and small trees, viburnum is sought after for three reasons: It's handsome, it's versatile and it's easy to grow. Truly a year-round shrub, it rewards you with flowers in spring or summer, appealing foliage in fall and berries from fall to winter. Grow in full sun or part shade.

FAVORITES: For summer flowers, look for Summer Snowflake. This viburnum produces white flowers in late spring and into summer.

7 Rose of Sharon

Hibiscus syriacus, Zones 5 to 9

When other flowers are spent, this late bloomer becomes a generous source of energy for hummingbirds. A member of the hibiscus family, it bears charming trumpet-shaped flowers that bloom from late summer through midautumn. In optimal conditions, including moist, well-draining soil and lots of sunshine, rose of Sharon can climb to 10 feet or more.

FAVORITES: We love the classic rose of Sharon, but two new cultivars introduced by Minier Nursery in France are really getting our attention, too: Tahiti, with deep pinkish-purple blooms, and Fiji, with unique semidouble fading blooms and dark red centers.

8 Crape myrtle

Lagerstroemia indica, Zones 7 to 9

Crape myrtle is a year-round belle in the South, where it thrives in the warmth and blooms from July to September. The spectacular flowers won't stop attracting butterflies, bees and hummingbirds. You can even remove the first wave of flowers to encourage a second bloom. Grow this heat-tolerant beauty in full sun, and it might get to be 10 feet or more.

FAVORITES: Purple Magic is a new crape myrtle that is considered a semidwarf variety, with clusters of dark purple blooms. It's a champion grower, bred for resistance to leaf spot and powdery mildew.

9 Summersweet

Clethra alnifolia, Zones 4 to 9

While it often flies under the radar, summersweet is a trustworthy summer bloomer that beckons butterflies and hummingbirds. (In fact, one cultivar is so popular it has hummingbird in the name.) Grow summersweet in full sun to partial shade. Blooms emerge in midsummer; even when the flowers fade, you'll still get pretty fall color from the foliage. This is one unfamiliar shrub you'll want to take a chance on.

FAVORITES: Hummingbird Summersweet is a cultivar with wonderful, fragrant flowers and compact growth. As the name promises, hummingbirds will flock to your yard for its abundant blossoms.

10 Hydrangea

Hydrangea, Zones 3 to 10

Gardeners have relied on hydrangeas for years to provide showy summer color. Easy to care for, they happily flower even in partial shade. Bigleaf hydrangeas (*Hydrangea macrophylla*) are ideal for mild climates but usually won't flower in regions with cold winters. In those areas, try cultivars of sevenbark hydrangea (*Hydrangea arborescens*), which typically produce big white blooms.

FAVORITES: You'll find all sorts of new hydrangeas on the market. Among our favorites are the new pink Annabelle options—either the Invincibelle Spirit cultivar, or Bella Anna in the Endless Summer line.

Love hydrangeas?

They might be the most beloved summer-blooming shrub, so we wanted to help you figure out which type is right for you.

LIVE IN A COLD REGION? Go with the classic Annabelle (*Hydrangea arborescens*), with white blooms. It can even survive in Zone 3, and you'll love the huge blossoms.

HAVE HOT SUMMERS? Grow oakleaf hydrangea (*Hydrangea quercifolia*). They bloom best in these climates, and the foliage is attractive in fall.

WANT BLUE HYDRANGEAS? Also called mopheads (*Hydrangea macrophylla*), these are probably the most popular in home gardens. The blooms will be blue if your soil is naturally acidic or if you acidify it; otherwise they'll be pink. You can also grow them in partial shade.

hummer happenings

Your "bird tales" celebrate all things hummingbird.

Ruby-throated hummingbirds prefer to feed on orange or red flowers.

Wings Wide Open

I waited anxiously for most of spring, hoping to get hummingbirds at my feeder. Finally one pair arrived. Hoping to draw more in, I bought some potted plants and placed them around the feeder. As you can see, the effort was appreciated!

Marty Maynard
MARSHFIELD, MISSOURI

◀ Scratch That Itch

The hummingbirds in my backyard often sit on sunflower leaves, although the leaves look more like branches next to them! This squirt is just a youngster, but a feisty one. It sits on this leaf or one nearby and guards the feeder for itself, successfully chasing the older birds away. Of course, every now and then, even a tiny hummingbird must take time from guard duty to scratch an itch!

Sherri Woodbridge MEDFORD, OREGON

Desperately Seeking Service

While I was sitting in my living room at the front of the house, a ruby-throated hummingbird appeared at the window. This was unusual, since our feeder is in the backyard. I watched the bird hover and dart back and forth in front of the window for the longest time, as if it was trying to give me a message. Suddenly I remembered that its normally dependable feeder was soaking in the kitchen sink. I was impressed with this bird's determination to find a human to complain to about the poor service!

Lin Vickery
CHARLOTTE, NORTH CAROLINA

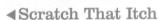

North America's feistiest hummingbird? The rufous!

◄ Rough & Ready!

The only time we normally see rufous hummingbirds in our part of Louisiana is when they winter here, which is what this little guy did in our yard. It was so fun and exciting watching him. He had a feeder all to himself, yet he was very protective of it, running off mockingbirds and cardinals alike.

When his juvenile coloration started to change, I knew he wouldn't be staying much longer. Sure enough, two days after the last of his bright adult feathers came in, he left for more northerly parts. I was lucky to have a couple of days to photograph him, and even more so to get this amazing shot!

Helena Reynolds
VENTRESS, LOUISIANA

Haute Hummingbird

Early every morning I walk around my backyard to see what garden chores I need to do. One day I wore a bright Hawaiian shirt with a pink hibiscus pattern, and a beautiful hummingbird—emerald green in color— approached. I froze, and the bird flew all around my shirt, studying each bloom. After flickering around me at a distance of about 10 inches, it must have decided that the flowers weren't real. Before it zipped away, it stopped about 3 inches from my face and hovered. I like to think it was giving me a nod of approval for my floral choice of clothing.

Sandra Muck
LINCOLN PARK, MICHIGAN

Hum for the Holiday

Our 8-foot artificial Christmas tree goes up in our protected patio each season. From there, we can fully enjoy it through our living room window without its crowding us out of the place.

Our winters are usually fairly mild, but a few years back temperatures dropped below freezing during the day. To our amazement, a hummingbird took up residence in our tree!

Having a colorful, living "ornament" keeping a sharp eye on its sugar-water feeder was something quite magical.

Floyd & Charlene Riley
SALEM, OREGON

Eastern North America has one breeding hummingbird— the ruby-throated.

Fingertip Feeder

After watching a video of a man hand-feeding hummingbirds in his backyard, I was instantly hooked and determined to try it. I hung my feeder right outside the window and waited until my hummingbirds were using it regularly. Then, while I sat comfortably in my house, I gradually put my hand out the window. They became used to me, so I tried removing the feeder, offering them some homemade nectar in a red measuring spoon. It didn't take long until they trusted me enough to land on my fingers, letting me take beautiful photos like this one.

Brooke Ligue PORTAGE, WISCONSIN

hummingbird heaven

According to the Cornell Lab of Ornithology, black-chinned hummingbirds aren't so much drawn to red as they are to the colors of recent nectar sources.

▲ Hooked On Photos

Though I've been feeding hummingbirds for many years, it was only recently that I finally decided to take some photos. This snapshot of an adult male black-chinned hummingbird was one of my first. It was a great moment to capture this little bird's expression, and thrilling to have many hummingbirds hovering around me before going to the feeders.
Gilberto Sanchez EL PASO, TEXAS

Nosy Little Hummingbird

We enjoy a huge influx of migratory birds every spring, especially our beloved hummingbirds. While I was walking the dog one morning, a black-chinned hummer approached me to investigate my red-and-white T-shirt. It buzzed closely, studying this new flower, even moving very near my face. I shut my eyes to better hear its buzzing. Suddenly, I felt a tickle in my nostril, and I jerked my head. The little bird had put its bill in my nose, mistaking it for a flower. Yes, I was pollinated by a hummingbird!
Mike Kotch CONCAN, TEXAS

◄ Handy Anna's

Each year we're lucky enough to see many young hummingbirds in our yard and to watch their colors mature. This handsome young male Anna's did quite a bit of posing for me last summer; I could find him pretty regularly on this sturdy perch among the crocosmia.
Kim Cunningham
LYNNWOOD, WASHINGTON

▲ Crowning Photo

My wife, Carol, and I love hummingbirds and love to travel, so it's no surprise that one of our favorite places to go is Costa Rica. A few years ago we visited a hummingbird garden close to the Monteverde Cloud Forest Reserve. We spent about two hours just sitting and watching 14 species feeding and displaying their gorgeous colors. I was fortunate enough to photograph this beautiful male green-crowned brilliant perched on a feeder.
Donald Ainley POPLAR BLUFF, MISSOURI

You'll find gorgeous Anna's hummingbirds, such as this young male, year-round on the West Coast.

did you know?

Learn more about these glittering little wonders with these amazing facts.

25 Hummingbirds have unusually large flight muscles, which make up about 25% of their body weight.

1,500 Hummingbirds have about 1,500 feathers.

14 The oldest hummingbird on record was 14 years old.

250 While resting, a hummingbird takes 250 breaths per minute.

50 Hummingbirds beat their wings about 50 times per second, so they appear as a blur.

make room for
hummingbirds
& butterflies

You don't need a lot of room to bring these beauties to your garden. Here are some easy solutions for small spaces.

BY MELINDA MYERS

CAROL L. EDWARDS

Female ruby-throat and monarch at butterfly bush

As a longtime small-space gardener, my motto has always been this: There's always room somewhere!

That includes finding a place for hummingbirds and butterflies. These beautiful fliers add color and life to any size landscape, balcony or container garden. So it's definitely worth the time and effort to create an inviting environment in the garden just for them. Here are my best tips for attracting hummingbirds and butterflies in a pocket-size space.

NEVER ENOUGH FLOWERS. Some of our favorites to bring in hummingbirds and butterflies are penstemon (left), petunias (center), zinnias (right, with a monarch) and coneflowers (below, with swallowtails).

Reducing your use of pesticides really will help you enjoy more views of hummingbirds and butterflies. Sure, chemicals might get rid of a few nuisances, but they can also injure or kill the wildlife you are trying to attract.

step 1: add flowers

Basic Blooms for Hummingbirds

You can apply any small-space planting strategy, as long as you include nectar-rich flowers like nicotiana, fuchsia, nasturtiums, salvia and other hummingbird favorites. And don't be afraid to use perennials, even in containers. Columbine, hostas, honeysuckle vine and penstemons will return each year to guarantee meals for your visitors.

Basic Blooms for Butterflies

Many hummingbird flowers will appeal to butterflies, too, but the latter are especially drawn to verbena, marigolds, zinnia, black-eyed Susans, gayfeather and coneflower. And don't forget food for the caterpillars. Parsley, dill and fennel add striking color and texture to the garden, while also flavoring your dinner and feeding caterpillars. Though the insects do eat the leaves, there will still be plenty for you to enjoy. More good news: These plants recover quickly when the caterpillars finish feeding.

step 2: add more flowers

Double Up on Plantings

Combine equally assertive plants for double the bloom or extended color in limited space. For instance, grape hyacinths planted in a ground cover of deadnettle can double the color in your late-spring or early-summer garden, enticing even more butterflies or hummingbirds. Two other options: Consider combining Blue Angel hostas and hakone grass in a shady corner, or plant colchicum with bugleweed.

Go Vertical

Growing skyward lets you pack lots of nectar-rich flowers, habitat and food for the caterpillars in very little space. Think about vines, espaliered trees, shrubs in containers and green walls.

Add Containers

Try some hummingbird, butterfly and caterpillar favorites in a container. Grow them alone in individual pots, or mix them up. Annuals are always an easy pick, but perennials, as well as small-scale trees and shrubs, will also work in pots. For best results in colder climates, grow container plants one or two zones hardier than usual in a weatherproof pot.

Extend Bloom Time

Increase the traffic in your small space by offering both early- and late-season bloomers. Add some cool-season annuals like pansies, stocks and snapdragons to your spring and fall garden. You might also consider growing native and ornamental grasses, which add motion and texture year-round. Many grasses provide nectar for butterflies, while the seeds feed a variety of birds and the whole plant can provide nesting material.

30 Surefire Hummingbird Flowers

SHRUBS, TREES AND VINES
Dropmore scarlet honeysuckle
Lilac
Mimosa
Morning glory
Rhododendron
Scarlet runner bean
Weigela

ANNUALS
Cleome
Flowering tobacco
Geranium
Hollyhock*
Impatiens
Lantana*
Nasturtium
Petunia
Zinnia

PERENNIALS
Asiatic lily
Bleeding heart
Canna*
Coral bells
Dahlia*
Daylily
Delphinium
Foxglove*
Gayfeather
Gladiola*
Hosta
Penstemon
Primrose
Yucca

*In some climates

step 3:
enjoy!

Put Out Resting Spots

Put a flat stone in your garden where butterflies can spread their wings and warm their bodies; they'll repay you with some perfect photo opportunities. For the hummingbirds, hang a perch near your sugar-water feeder.

Try Water Features

Add a puddle where the butterflies can gather and lap up a bit of moisture and salt. Sink a wide, shallow dish, flowerpot or bucket filled with sand into the soil. Keep it damp and wait for the party to begin. For hummingbirds, provide a mister or some sort of slow-moving water feature. Make your own, or look for small-scale fountains or other water features at your local garden center.

Plan a Great View

Be sure to place your containers and build your gardens where you can watch these charming visitors feed on your plants. Consider the views from inside your home looking out. A hanging basket near a kitchen or family room window can bring butterflies and hummingbirds within view. Think about including sitting areas near your garden, or moving containers closer to the seating you already have. Then you can relax and wait for the show to begin.

Get inspiration from this container of phlox, petunias and butterfly flower.

A giant swallowtail and a white peacock share space at coneflowers.

Grow hibiscus in containers for a tropical look and to attract birds such as this female ruby-throat.

Look for dozens of types of noninvasive butterfly bush on the market these days.

take 5

Melinda put together quick "top 5" lists to help you plan your garden.

5 HUMMINGBIRD FAVORITES

- Salvia guaranitica
- Verbena bonariensis
- Phlox
- Fuchsia
- Cuphea

5 BUTTERFLY FAVORITES

- Pentas
- Lantana
- Tithonia
- Zinnia
- Lo & Behold butterfly bush

5 CATERPILLAR FAVORITES

- Parsley
- Butterfly weed
- Cornflower
- Sunflower
- Snapdragon

5 VINES FOR BUTTERFLIES

- Passion vine
- Pipevine
- Mexican flame vine
- Black-eyed Susan vine
- Clematis

5 VINES FOR HUMMINGBIRDS

- Hyacinth bean vine
- Climbing nasturtium
- Cypress vine
- Trumpet vine
- Trumpet honeysuckle

glad you asked!

Birding expert George Harrison answers your questions.

Female ruby-throated hummingbirds feed insects to their young because insects are a good source of protein.

Female and juvenile ruby-throats, like this one, don't have the signature red throat.

▲ **I see hummingbirds flying to the blue spruce in my yard. What are they after?**
Loretta McClincy BELLEFONTE, PENNSYLVANIA

GEORGE: Besides nectar, hummingbirds also eat—and feed to their babies—small insects, which they gather from flowers, shrubs and trees. In the case of the blue spruce, not only are they finding insects there, but the sap the tree produces is a nourishing food for them. Often, yellow-bellied sapsuckers will drill holes in spruce trunks to release pools of sap. Hummingbirds feast on this treat also.

◄ **This is one of two hummingbirds that visit every September. Is it an immature male? At what age do hummingbirds get their full coloring?**
Lynn Smith LEAGUE CITY, TEXAS

GEORGE: Yes, the hummingbirds you're seeing are most likely immature male ruby-throats. By the time immature hummingbirds return to their nesting grounds in the U.S. in spring, they are in full adult plumage. The ones you've been seeing in fall were probably hatched a couple of months earlier and were migrating through your yard on their way for the first time to their wintering grounds in the tropics.

My hummingbirds always seem to leave in mid-September—and for the last month they're here, I see only females. Is this a normal pattern?
Carolyn Sweet
ROCHESTER, MASSACHUSETTS

GEORGE: The ruby-throated hummingbirds you see in the last month before they migrate are all juveniles that look like females. Adult hummingbirds depart before their young do, leaving the offspring to grow and fatten up for their first long flight to the tropics. The amazing part is that these youngsters don't fly in flocks. They go solo on a path they have never flown before, many of them across the Gulf of Mexico into South America.

I have two hummingbird feeders in my yard but no hummingbirds. How can I encourage them to visit?
Cassidy Albrecht STEWART, MINNESOTA

GEORGE: A surefire way to attract hummingbirds is to plant red flowers. Almost any red bloom—geraniums, impatiens, petunias, bee balm (pictured at top), honeysuckle, fuchsia—will entice them to visit a

garden. Once you get their attention with the flowers, you can install feeders among the blooms and get them hooked on sugar water. Then you'll be able to move the feeders wherever you want them.

I noticed a hummingbird nest in a bare tree last winter. Will a hummingbird use it next year?
Margaret Saiauskie
GLEN MILLS, PENNSYLVANIA

GEORGE: It is not likely. Hummingbirds build a new nest each year, and those that have two broods a year build a new nest for the second brood. There is at least one report of a female ruby-throated hummingbird feeding fledglings from one nest while incubating eggs in a second nest. Like many other birds, hummingbirds will

return to the same nesting grounds year after year and will build nests in or around the same trees, but they will not use an old nest.

By feeding hummingbirds, how much are we helping them? If I didn't feed these little birds, would it matter?
Lynda Franco BUFFALO, MISSOURI

GEORGE: If you totally stopped feeding the hummingbirds, they would survive just fine. Studies have shown that wild birds glean only a small percentage of their daily food from feeders. I'm sure that there are others in your neighborhood who would pick up the slack should you stop feeding. Don't worry about your birds becoming dependent on your feeders. We feed birds for our own pleasure, not for the health and prosperity of the birds.

FAQ

"When should I start and stop feeding hummingbirds?"

GEORGE: Early May is a good time to hang out your hummingbird feeders—except in the South, where migratory hummers begin tapping sugar-water feeders in early April. And don't hurry to take them down in fall. It's a myth that if you keep your feeders up, the hummingbirds won't migrate. When you leave your feeders in place through migration season, you'll catch any late travelers as they fly through your area.

Ruby-throated hummingbird at coneflower
Photo by Carol L. Edwards

Snowy-bellied hummingbird
Photo by David Tipling/Getty Images

Blue-throated hummingird
Photo by Terry Lairmore

Broad-tailed hummingbird
Photo by Gary Botello

Ruby-throated hummingbird
Photo by Steve and Dave Maslowski

CHAPTER 3

DIY Backyard

Take pride in do-it-yourself upgrades you can enjoy for years to come. Fit easy projects into even your busiest weekends. Create everything from fun feeders and houses to a stackable garden and solar-powered fountain.

GRACE NATOLI SHELDON/RDA-MKE

all in a day's work

Time-strapped gardeners can complete these
quick and easy ideas before the sun goes down.

BY CRYSTAL RENNICKE

*paint
containers*

_make
bright
cushions_

Wouldn't it be wonderful if we could spend countless hours tackling our garden to-do's? In reality, while we balance careers, family and household chores, our garden aspirations are often left unfulfilled.

Yet even the busiest of us can spare a day, an afternoon or an hour now and then. And in even 60 minutes of time, you can accomplish a lot! These ideas are simple enough to complete in a day or less—and they won't bust your budget, either.

If You Have an Hour

ADD FLAIR TO YOUR CHAIRS. A quick fix for dull outdoor furniture is a simple coat or two of paint. Have fun with it—no need to use matching colors. Lively hues work well in the backyard, especially near vibrant flower combos. For an extra pop of color, prop bright pillows on your chairs; buy them or make them from old fabric scraps.

SET UP A READING NOOK. Have a quiet, tucked-away place in the backyard? Set up a tranquil reading space with a comfy chair in a shady spot. No shade? Make your own with a homemade canopy or a stylish umbrella. Arrange an assortment of fragrant flowers in a container and place it nearby.

_create a
reading
nook_

*install a
window box*

*add a
raised bed*

CREATE QUICK CONTAINERS. For instant impact, start with a colorful container, or paint a pot you already own. Try out-of-the-ordinary containers like crates, old drawers, galvanized tubs, chairs or anything with drainage holes. Establish a theme with your plant picks: Make a purple container with pansies, petunias or heliotrope, or a butterfly garden with pentas, purple coneflower and salvia.

BRIGHTEN YOUR NIGHTLIFE. If you entertain outdoors in the evening, paint a few containers with glow-in-the-dark acrylic paint. They'll brighten up your backyard in an unexpected way. Hang mason jars from tree branches with colorful ribbons. Fill them with candles for a fun way to light up the night.

MAKE YOUR MARK. Add a personal touch to your garden beds with homemade plant markers. Use objects you have around the house: wooden spoons, paint sticks, clothespins, painted rocks. These ordinary items become eye-catching when you add a little creativity.

FILL IN BARE SPOTS. If you have an empty fence or a blank wall, make it pretty by hanging outdoor art or flat-backed planters filled with colorful plants.

Day Projects for the Birds
Treat the birds to these projects that take less than an hour to complete.
• Put a few decorative plates or shallow bowls filled with water around the yard for some fun and budget-friendly birdbaths.
• Dried gourds, empty cans or even boots make excellent birdhouses.
• Just about anything can serve as a bird feeder. Old mugs, muffin tins, decorative plates or bowls—the list is endless.

If You Have an Afternoon
ELEVATE BORING FLOORING. A concrete patio or a plain deck floor provides an opportunity in the form of a blank canvas. If you're artistic, try painting a "rug" on your deck. Stain or paint a stamped concrete patio for a high-end look. Or simply buy a weatherproof rug to add some homey comfort to your outdoor space.

INSTALL SOLAR LIGHTS. They're simple to install and add a lot of appeal to the nighttime garden. While you're at it, plant a few white flowers nearby, such as white alyssum, lantana and moonflower. They'll make your garden glow even more.

*make mosaic
stepping-stones*

spruce up your entry

GROW A WATER GARDEN. Find a watertight pot, or add a waterproof liner to a large container, like a whiskey barrel. Put pavers or bricks inside at varying heights and add potted water plants and accents like grasses and flowering plants. Install a pump to get the water moving for soothing sounds that also attract birds.

DANGLE A DIY CHANDELIER. Fancy up outdoor dinner parties with a homemade chandelier to hang above your patio table. Add your own touches to an old chandelier base—jars filled with candles, jewels, ornaments or beads. If you don't have a base, make your own. We've seen readers fashion chandeliers out of Christmas lights attached to an umbrella frame or a spray-painted hula-hoop. Brilliant!

PIECE TOGETHER MOSAICS. If you've retired your old bowling ball, repurpose it into garden art. Glue on tiles, flat-backed marbles, coins or mirrors; let it all dry and add grout or paint on a design. Or if your plain stepping-stones could use a makeover, add mortar and place mosaics on top.

If You Have a Day

ENHANCE YOUR ENTRY. To spruce up the yard with some dimension, install an arbor or gate at the entrance of your garden or dress up your front steps with flowers. Plant fragrant climbing vines, such as sweet autumn clematis, climbing rose or wisteria, or arrange some containers at each entrance.

RAISE A VEGGIE GARDEN. Planting a vegetable garden is simple when you use a raised bed. With just a few pieces of lumber, soil and compost, you've set the stage for growing your favorite veggies. For an added touch, paint the wood a fun color to pick up hues you already have in your garden.

MULCH AND EDGE BEDS. Make your garden beds look polished with mulch. If you don't already have a barrier (or if your edging needs an upgrade), it takes only a little while to edge your beds. Use bricks, rocks or pavers for a finished look that'll also make mowing much easier.

MAKE A RAIN BARREL. If you don't want to buy a pricey rain barrel, it isn't time-consuming to make or decorate your own. If the blue barrel look isn't your thing, you can easily paint it to make it more appealing. We've also seen readers transform whiskey barrels and garbage cans into attractive rain barrels.

ADD WOW TO YOUR WINDOWS. An underused portion of the house lies underneath your windows. Installing window boxes instantly adds charm and value to your home. Make them with leftover lumber, then add your own personal touches and no-fuss flowers.

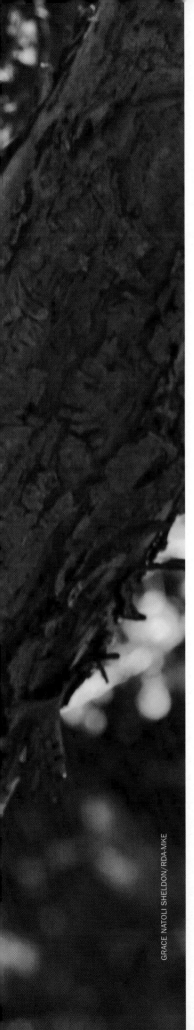

soda bottle bird feeder

Create a feeding station that positively pops for the seedeaters in your backyard.

BY TAMI COVEY

I never throw away glass. I'm a glass artist, and you just never know when a plate, jar or even a soda bottle might make the perfect addition to your next project.

This crafty bird feeder cost me just a few dollars, and now I'm sharing my secret with you. All you'll need are patience and a couple of hours to make your own. Then sit back and watch while the birds enjoy their treats!

supplies

- Glass soda bottle with cap
- ¼-in. threaded steel rod, 12 in. long
- 7¼ x 7½-in. turnbuckle with two eyebolts
- Loctite glue
- Chicken feeder
- Washer
- ¼-in. threaded wing nut
- G-hook
- 1-in. diamond drill bit
- ½-in. regular twist drill bit

STEP 1. Glass soda bottles aren't hard to find these days. Mexican Coca-Cola is usually sold this way, and it's readily available across the United States. Once you have the bottle (I used a 1-liter bottle), find something to hold the neck to keep it in place. I find the garbage disposal in my kitchen sink ideal for this.

STEP 2. Next, under running water, use a 1-in. diamond drill bit to make a hole in the bottom of the bottle. This is the most difficult part of the project. It's important to keep your drill bit and glass cool by immersing them in water; overheating can break the bottle and even ruin your bit. Start at an angle, gently holding the drill bit in place. Once the drill bit has made a groove in the glass, straighten the bit up

so that it hits all sides of the hole evenly. Run your drill at a slow speed to start out, speeding up as the bit becomes deeper, then slowing down toward the end. Once you've made the hole, you may need to file the sharp edges; an emery board will do.

STEP 3. With the ½-in. drill bit, drill a hole in the center of the chicken feeder and Coke bottle cap.

STEP 4. Connect the turnbuckle and the steel rod by removing one of the eye hooks from the turnbuckle and screwing the rod into place. Once you've determined that you have the correct length, you can use a drop or two of Loctite to keep it from moving, but don't do this until you have put it together successfully at least once.

STEP 5. Taking out the other eye hook, place it through the drilled hole in the bottle cap and screw it back into the turnbuckle. The eye of the eyebolt will be on top of the cap for your hanging hook to thread through.

STEP 6. Feed the steel rod through the top of the bottle, past the hole in the bottom of the bottle and then through the hole in the chicken feeder. Firmly press the bottle cap down on the lip of the bottle.

STEP 7. Holding the feeder upside down, place the washer over the threaded rod. Last, screw the wing nut in place.

STEP 8. Attach a hook. I use a G-hook, but you may choose a different type depending on where you want to hang it.

STEP 9. Once you're ready to fill your bird feeder, simply take the bottom off, fill the feeder with your favorite seed and reattach the bottom.

STEP 10. Finally, find the best place in your yard to hang your creation so that you and the birds can enjoy the perfect Coke date!

GRACE NATOLI SHELDON/RDA-MKE

stackable garden

Create a vertical blooming masterpiece with old dresser drawers.

BY ALISON AUTH

5147

I love drawers. Small ones, big ones, skinny ones, shallow ones—I'll take them any way I can find them. So whenever I discover a big old ugly dresser in an alley or a thrift store, all I can think about is what I'm going to do with the drawers.

Here's a nifty way to put them to use as a vertical garden wall. Whether you place it in your garden, or on a front porch as I've done here, it will add interest and color to your space.

supplies

- Drawers
- Handles
- Wood scraps
- Screws and screwdriver
- Drill
- Sandpaper
- Exterior-grade paint and primer
- Plants
- Potting soil
- Finish nails, brads or staples (optional)
- Lawn-and-leaf bags (optional)
- House numbers (optional)

STEP 1. Stack the drawers so that you have a solid foundation and ample planting spaces. I used two matching drawers screwed together on the bottom to provide a wide, sturdy base. From there, I cantilevered all the boxes in opposite directions, using the center of the bottom boxes as my visual guide. Not only is this attractive, but balancing the drawers this way provides stability.

STEP 2. Once you know how you're going to arrange the drawers, make feet out of wood scraps and screw them onto the bottom drawer or drawers. For my feet, I used a salt-treated 4-by-4 cut into 3-in. lengths. If using two drawers for the bottom, screw those together first, then attach the feet, including a fifth one for support where the two base drawers meet. Adding feet ensures that water will drain freely away from the unit, preventing rot. Just make sure the feet are chunky enough to support the weight of the unit.

STEP 3. Next, drill drainage holes in the bottoms of all the drawers. The size of the hole is not critical; a drill bit of about a quarter inch worked for me. You'll need about 10 holes per drawer to get good drainage.

STEP 4. Sand, prime and paint each drawer individually with exterior-grade coatings. You can paint the inside of the drawers as well, or you can shellac them to seal the wood to prevent decay. You can also leave the interiors unfinished and line them with plastic lawn-and-leaf bags if you prefer, but coating them in some way will definitely prolong their life.

STEP 5. Now is a good time to attach any decorative handles, house numbers or other embellishments to the drawer faces. You also may want to experiment with the placement of the drawers at this point, or draw your planned design on paper first.

STEP 6. Starting from the bottom, attach each drawer to the one below. I found the easiest way to do this was to cut a piece of scrap wood the width of the lower drawer to support the drawer that will go on top. Secure the support board to the inside of the lower drawer with screws. Rest the next drawer on top of this support board and the perimeter of the drawer below, and then secure it with screws, brads, pneumatic staples or finish nails—whatever is readily available and works for you. Repeat this process with all of the drawers.

STEP 7. To ensure that your drawer garden won't pull apart as soon as you move it, cut at least two lengths of wood to the height of the finished unit (not including the legs); a 1- x 3-in. or 1- x 4-in. strip of wood is ideal. Screw these to the back of your unit, making sure to include each drawer. This provides rigid bracing and additional strength to the finished piece.

STEP 8. Time to plant! You can put potted plants in your unit or take them out of the pots and plant directly in the drawers. I found a mixture of upright grasses, hanging vines and dramatic blooms to be a lovely combination.

Gardening at Any Cost
How to plan a garden, no matter your budget.

Getting Started

FREE Check websites such as *craigslist.org* or *freecycle.org* for local ads offering free soil and mulch for your garden beds and containers. Remember, though, that "free" may come with a price. Go to extra lengths to make sure you're not transferring bad or diseased soil and mulch.

LOW-COST Contact your local extension office, where they may know of nearby sources of inexpensive soil and mulch. You can also call landscaping companies or tree services to see if they sell discount mulch. Some may even deliver, so you'll just need to invest in a wheelbarrow.

SPLURGE There's no shame in throwing your hands in the air and declaring defeat. Sometimes you don't have the time or energy to dig that new garden bed, lay mulch and keep up with the weeding. Hire someone to do the dirty work while you reap the rewards.

Growing Seeds

FREE Have a seed swap among friends and neighbors. Or check local events listings to see if there's already one going on near you. You can also join an online group, such as *Birds & Blooms'* Seed Swap forum. Visit our online community to meet others who want to trade.

LOW-COST At $40, the Deep Root Seed Starting System from *gardeners.com* is a bargain. It has deep cells that encourage a better root system, and you can use it year after year. Bonus: It's self-watering!

SPLURGE Providing the right kind of light helps your young seedlings grow healthy and strong. Check out *burpee.com* for a selection of grow-light kits. For $325, you can pick up the Single Light Glow'n Grow Light Garden Kit. It's lightweight, free-standing and portable, and will hold standard-size grow trays.

Planting Time

FREE You needn't go far for freebies. Look in your backyard for plants you can take cuttings from and bulbs you can divide, or gather friends and neighbors for a plant exchange.

LOW-COST Search online to see if the Master Gardener program near you has an annual plant sale. Generally, many of the plants on sale come straight from the gardens of these experts, who will be on hand to answer questions.

SPLURGE Take an afternoon, visit your favorite nursery (you know—the fancy one!), and buy something you've always wanted to try. If you save in other areas, the price will sting a little less. Go ahead, you deserve it.

Be a Savvy Shopper
When I find hanging baskets on sale for $1.99, I buy them instead of purchasing separate plants. Then I take out all the plants and distribute them among my planters for more color and variety. It's less expensive this way, and I always have the basket to use as needed.
Carol Ely FAIRBURY, ILLINOIS

muffin tin bird feeder

Take a break from baking, and feed your feathered friends instead.

BY BRIAN CARLISLE

Before you buy a new birdhouse or feeder, consider making your own with a little creative upcycling. I've been doing it for years. Teakettles, license plates, coffeepots, pans, old utensils and knobs are just a few of the items I use in my designs.

My latest project is this muffin tin bird feeder, which lets you offer an array of different foods in one handy holder. You probably have most of the supplies already or can get them for practically nothing. (I spent less than $20 on all of my materials.) Here are some simple steps you can follow to make your own.

The supplies

supplies

- **Muffin tin**
- **Pan, lid or board for roof**
- **Metal hole punch or drill**
- **8 key rings**
- **Jack chain**
- **Drawer handle or other hanger (optional)**
- **Metal screws (optional)**
- **Brass bell or other counterweight (optional)**

STEP 1. Mark the places (a) where you want to drill the holes for the corners of the muffin tin and of the pan, lid or board that will be your roof.

STEP 2. Use either a metal hole punch or a drill bit to make holes (b) in the muffin tin and the roof big enough for the key rings.

STEP 3. Mark spots for a small hole at the bottom center of each cup of the muffin tin for drainage. Then punch or drill the holes (c), making sure they're not so big that your birdseed will fall through.

STEP 4. Run the key rings through the holes at the corners of the muffin tin and the roof (d).

STEP 5. If your roof doesn't already have a handle for hanging, decide how you want to hang the feeder. I like using found items such as drawer or luggage handles, but even a simple eyebolt will work. Making sure the handle is positioned in the center, screw it to the roof (e).

STEP 6. Attach four lengths of jack chain to hold everything together. You'll probably find it best to use lengths of 8 in. or shorter between the muffin tin and the roof. You can use even shorter lengths if you plan to feed only small songbirds.

STEP 7. You'll probably want to hang a counterweight from the bottom to offset the weight of larger birds, which will reduce the tossing of birdseed when the big guys come in for a landing. You can use anything from a large garden faucet handle to a big handbell or even an old doorknob. Test a few things out until you find one that works for you. Drill a hole in the center of the muffin tin. Then, using an eyebolt or a plumbing pipe hanger and another length of chain, attach the counterweight (f). Note: If you intend for only small birds to use your feeder, you probably won't need a counterweight.

STEP 8. Have some fun by decorating your finished bird feeder any way you like. For a funky look, try hanging small objects from the chains or the corners of the muffin tin or roof; I've used vintage skeleton keys. What a good excuse to go rummaging at a garage sale this weekend!

We placed this fountain in dappled sun to get a good photo, but remember, full sun is best long-term.

bringing solar to the garden

Create your own solar-powered fountain in less than an hour.
And look, it's a planter, too!

BY VICKI SCHILLEMAN

Last year, I saw a picture of a fountain that doubled as a planter. I fell in love with the concept, but I couldn't find directions for making it. So I came up with my own design. And while I was at it, I made it solar-powered, too.

This is a really simple project. The most vital step is picking a sunny location for your pots, before you start. This is important for two reasons. First, the fountain will work only when the sun is shining directly on the solar panels. Second, once the fountain is assembled, it'll probably be too heavy to move!

So, pick up some pretty pots and a solar fountain pump this spring—you'll have a new water feature and planter for your yard in no time.

supplies

- **2 pots of different sizes**
- **Platform to go in larger pot**
- **Soil**
- **Plants**
- **Solar-powered fountain unit (see Step 6)**

STEP 1. This project starts at the garden center where you choose your containers. In the photo on page 98, you can see that the fountain features a smaller pot nestled in a larger one. (The third pot visible behind the large one is not necessary.) While you're at the store, test out different pots to see how they look together. You'll want to make sure the proportions are right before you get them home.

STEP 2. If your containers have drainage holes, you'll need to plug the holes of the smaller one, which will hold water for the fountain. I used cork to plug the hole and then covered it with heavy-duty plastic using hot glue. You don't have to use cork, but choose a material that won't deteriorate. Make sure all the edges of the plastic are glued down and everything is dry. To check for leaks, pour a pitcher of water into the pot. And if your large pot doesn't have drainage holes, drill a few in the bottom so your soil won't be soggy.

STEP 3. Place the platform in the larger pot. The one in the photo uses a wooden platform fitted about halfway down into the container. If you're using round pots, you could also use an Ups-A-Daisy planter insert, which you can check out at *ups-a-daisy.com.*

STEP 4. Place the smaller pot in the larger one, setting it firmly on the platform insert. Make sure it's level and secure. Then fill the space between the pots with potting soil.

STEP 5. Slowly add water to the top pot, making sure the pot stays level and safely seated in the soil. When the small pot is full, plant your flowers or greenery in the large pot and pack the soil tightly around the small pot to keep it secure. Water the plants until the water seeps out the drainage hole of the bottom pot, adding soil to the pot as necessary.

STEP 6. Finally, unpack and assemble the solar fountain and place it in the small pot. I chose a self-contained unit that uses solar panels floating on the water. Other models have solar panels that are connected to the pump with wires, with the solar panel generally stuck into the ground some distance away. The latter, which are designed mostly for ponds, won't work as well for this project.

STEP 7. As the water evaporates, add more. And don't forget to water your plants, too.

ANYTHING IS FAIR GAME TO UPCYCLE— red wagons, rusty wheelbarrows, old pans, etc. They'll all make perfect containers once you add drainage holes. Hunt through those summer rummage sales and hit up thrift stores for container inspiration. Baskets, coffeepots and even an old set of dresser drawers can all work.

mossy birdhouse

Treat your backyard guests to deluxe digs with this natural-looking house.

With its mossy green covering and pieces of driftwood and wood bark, this birdhouse is truly inspired by Mother Nature. Set it on a patio table or on a shelf under a garden porch, or hang it from a tree.

supplies

- Birdhouse (homemade or store-bought)
- Oil-based exterior spray paint
- 80-grit sandpaper
- Self-adhesive moss sheet, available from craft stores
- Loose artificial moss
- Driftwood sticks and small wood bark chips
- Glue
- Staples

STEP 1. Paint the birdhouse and let it dry. Lightly sand.

STEP 2. Cut the self-adhesive moss sheet to size, peel off the backing, and apply to the house one panel at a time. Use a utility knife to cut a slit in the moss over the front entrance hole, then push the moss through to the inside with your fingers.

STEP 3. Glue loose artificial moss into any gaps, then staple the moss around the edges of the birdhouse to attach it securely.

STEP 4. Drill holes in driftwood sticks, then nail the pieces in place on the roof. Apply a generous amount of glue to the roof and cover with loose moss and small pieces of bark, pressing the moss down firmly to ensure that it sticks.

BIRDHOUSE: CAROLINE ARBER/HANDMADE BIRDHOUSES AND FEEDERS; "GROW": ANNA GARFORTH

CRAFTING WITH MOSS

Here are a few more ways to get creative with moss.

COVER WOODEN LETTERS with moss and hang them on your door as a welcome to your home.

ADD GREENERY to a home or an office by making a moss terrarium.

USE MOSS TO FILL IN THE SPACES on a vertical succulent wall or a piece of wall art.

REUSE OLD COASTERS by covering them with moss. They'll be a nice addition to patio furniture.

THIS PROJECT IS COURTESY OF *Handmade Birdhouses and Feeders* by Michele McKee-Orsini, with photographs by Caroline Arber. It is published by CICO Books. For more information, visit *cicobooks.com*.

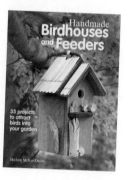

serve
multiple
kinds of
food

bird feeder buffet

Give your backyard birds a variety of food choices with this DIY feeder.

Set out a smorgasbord of tasty treats for your bird friends. A screw through the middle is a handy place to hang an apple, orange or corncob, and the double tray on the bottom will hold different types of birdseed.

supplies

- One 6-ft. x 5½-in. x ½-in. cedar fence board
- One 6-ft. x 3½-in. x ½-in. cedar fence board
- Waterproof glue
- 1-in. finishing nails or galvanized wire nails
- Drill with ⅛- and ⁵⁄₁₆-in. bits
- 1¼-in.-long exterior screws
- Two 4-in. lengths of ⁵⁄₁₆-in. dowel for perches
- 2½-in.-long exterior screw
- Heavy black wire
- 80-grit sandpaper (optional)
- Exterior craft paint (optional)
- Water-based exterior varnish (optional)

STEP 1. For the center piece, cut an 11¼-in. length from the 5½-in.-wide board. Cut a 1-in. hole in the piece about 8 inches from the bottom end. Cut each corner off the top end at a 45-degree angle to form a 90-degree peak. Set aside the cutoff triangles.

STEP 2. Cut two 6-in. pieces off the 5½-in.-wide board for the roof pieces. Bevel one short end of each piece at 45 degrees. Glue and nail the roof pieces together along the beveled edges.

STEP 3. Lay the remaining 5½-in.-wide board horizontally. Put the assembled roof at one end and draw a line at the other edge of the roof. Cut along the line; this will be the buffet floor.

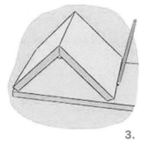

3.

STEP 4. Glue and nail the center piece to the middle of the floor. Glue and nail one of the cutoff triangles to each side of the center piece to give it extra stability.

STEP 5. From the 3½-in. board, cut two pieces the same length as the floor. Glue and nail one piece to each side of the floor. Then cut two pieces the same length as the front and back of the floor, including the sides you've just attached. Glue and nail them to the front and back of the floor to complete the feeder.

4.

STEP 6. Using a ⅛-in. bit, drill small holes at each corner and in the center of each side of the feeder, then drill in 1¼-in.-long screws to ensure that the sides are firmly fixed in place.

STEP 7. Using a ⁵⁄₁₆-in. bit, drill two holes in the center piece about a fourth of the way down from the roof and 1 in. from the sides. Gently tap in the dowel perches. Using the ⅛-in. bit, drill a small hole below the perches, then drill in a 2½-in. exterior screw to hang fruit slices.

5.

7.

STEP 8. If desired, sand the roof and the outside of the feeder and paint them; when completely dry, apply varnish. Leave the center piece and the interior of the feeder box unpainted for the birds' safety.

STEP 9. Using the ⅛-in. bit, drill a small hole in the center of each side of the roof, then drill a 1¼-in. exterior screw partway into each hole. Wrap the end of a 24-in. length of heavy black wire around each screw; tighten the screw to secure. Wrap the other end of each wire several times around a paintbrush to form a twist, then wrap the twisted wire around a hook or link swivel to make a secure hook for hanging.

9.

STEP 10. Using the ⅛-in. bit, drill a hole through each corner of the roof. Twist the center of a 12-in. length of black wire, then feed the ends through each hole from underneath, and twist the ends several times to secure; this forms another perch for the birds.

10.

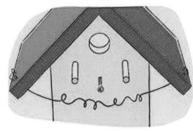

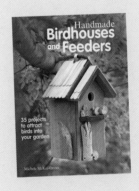

THIS PROJECT IS COURTESY OF
Handmade Birdhouses and Feeders by Michele McKee-Orsini, with photographs by Caroline Arber. It is published by CICO Books. For more information, visit *cicobooks.com*.

This example (also shown in the photos on page 105) uses a basket with planting holes in the sides (from *kinsmangarden.com*). Side planting gives a basket instant fullness.

1-2-3 container garden

You're only three steps away from season-long blooms with this easy container method.

BY PAMELA CRAWFORD

Containers should be easy. I've believed this since I first started planting flowers in pots and writing books on the subject. So, when the editors of *Birds & Blooms* asked if I could write an article on simplifying container gardening, I knew it was a perfect fit. I've used this three-step system in all four of my container books, and I hope you find it useful as well. With a growing market of plants and pots, there has never been a better time for more container gardens.

STEP 1.
Choose a Centerpiece.
A centerpiece is a plant placed in the middle of an arrangement. I usually choose the centerpiece first, since it becomes the focal point. I like to make my choice at the garden center and carry it around on a shopping cart to see which other plants I like with it. Some of my tips for choosing a centerpiece:
• The centerpiece should remain taller than the surrounding plants.
• Use a centerpiece with a different texture than the surrounding plants.
• Some of my favorite centerpieces include caladiums, blue salvia, giant coleus, grasses, pentas, Persian shield and showy ti plants.

STEP 2.
Choose Side and Edge Plants.
Once you have chosen your centerpiece, look for smaller plants with rootballs of 3 to 4½ inches to place around the centerpiece. Trust your instincts. See which combinations make you smile. Some of my tips for choosing side and edge plants:
• Limit the number of different plants you choose. It's easiest to work with just a few types.
• Stick to mounding plants in the beginning.
• Alternate plants throughout the basket. This way you won't use too many plants of one kind in a certain area, and your basket can grow evenly.

STEP 3.
Choose the Planting Plan.
There are thousands of ways to arrange plants in containers. My three favorite methods:
• The 1-2-3 planting plan alternates plants around the sides and edge, accenting the centerpiece.
• The layered planting plan has the sides in one pattern and the edge in another, with the centerpiece coming out the top.
• The striped planting plan is similar to the 1-2-3 plan, except you place the same plant above itself, just on a different layer.

   You can apply this three-step system to any container. Try it with the example pictured on these pages.

welcome Wildlife

Turn your place into home sweet home for winged creatures of all kinds. Put out the welcome mat using clever gardening secrets and planting tricks. Keep everything budget-friendly with thrifty ideas that'll save you money.

MARIE READ

create a bird-friendly
backyard

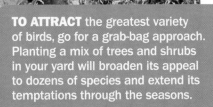

TO ATTRACT the greatest variety of birds, go for a grab-bag approach. Planting a mix of trees and shrubs in your yard will broaden its appeal to dozens of species and extend its temptations through the seasons.

Serviceberry trees attract many birds, like this male indigo bunting.

A few clever gardening tricks will turn your yard into a bird haven.

BY SALLY ROTH

Mulberries are tempting to rose-breasted grosbeaks.

Try your hand at birdscaping, and you'll quickly learn that landscaping is for the birds—literally! Planting with birds in mind pays off fast, bringing more birds, more kinds of birds and longer visits from your friends. It's easy, too. All it takes is looking at your yard from a bird's point of view.

Birdscaping Basics

You'll have greater success at attracting your favorites when you realize two things: Finding food and not getting eaten are the two biggest issues for birds.

Sure, you can just put out a tempting spread at the feeders, and birds will come. But to get them to linger, and maybe grace your place with a nest come spring, you'll need to make them feel safe, both while they're eating and while they're moving about the yard. This is the backbone of birdscaping.

"The more plants, the better" is my motto. A yard that's chock-full of different trees, shrubs, grasses and vines, plus the usual flower beds, is what brings in the birds. One that's mostly lawn won't get many customers at all.

You might think food is the best way to get birds to your yard—and it is. Food is exactly what they're after on all those plants, including insects in incredible numbers and any tempting berries or fruit. But surprisingly, seed probably comes last when it comes to attracting birds.

Observe and Learn

You can learn a lot about planning for birds just by watching them in their natural surroundings. Observe them in your yard, and you'll see that very few of them spend time out in the open. Most birds move from one clump of plants to another. They alight in trees, gather in bushes or scoot through the garden looking for food. The sheltering branches or stems protect them from the hungry eyes of hawks, prowling cats and any of the other critters that are only too happy to

8 ways to pinch those pennies

1. Dig suckers from lilacs, forsythia, weigela, serviceberry, shrub roses and any other multiple-stemmed plants you like, then transplant them to new homes.

2. Trees and shrubs cost less at garden centers than nurseries. Selection is often limited, and plants may not be as nicely shaped or as big, but the money savings may get you three or four plants instead of just one.

3. Look for free or cheap plants on *craigslist.com* or *freecycle.com*. Early birds get the worm.

4. Scour the bulletin boards at local supermarkets and other community hubs, and post your own notice for "Free Plants Wanted."

5. Bare-root shrubs are a bargain. Look for bramble fruits, forsythia, hedge plants and roses in bags rather than pots.

6. Shop end-of-season sales to save a bundle.

7. Scout the "sad sack" section of your favorite nursery and garden center for damaged but salvageable plants at cut-rate prices.

8. Treasure every bird-planted tree seedling you find in your yard; transplant them while they're still small.

The Perfect Plant

You can find hundreds of specific plants to attract birds, but how do you get started finding them? This general list will steer you in the right direction.

- Native trees or shrubs
- Flowering crabapples, hawthorns or Callery pears
- Fruit trees or bushes
- Junipers
- Pines, spruces
- Other flowering trees and shrubs

Cardinals are attracted to flowering trees, like this weeping cherry, because of the insects that visit the blossoms.

dine on a dove, sparrow or chickadee.

So think like a wary bird and set up stepping-stones of shrubs, trees, grasses and flower beds. Go horizontal with corridors of plants so birds can move easily about your yard. A hedge of mixed berry bushes is irresistible to bluebirds, thrashers, catbirds and other friends. Groups of shrubs with just a hop, skip and jump between them are also great.

But think vertically, too, because birds move up and down as well as sideways. You can shoehorn in a surprising amount of cover by layering small trees, shrubs, ferns and ground covers near big trees, and by adding an arbor or trellises for vines and roses.

Thinking like a bird instantly reveals the benefits of including ornamental grasses, roses and other shrubs, as well as small trees, in your flower beds. Your backyard will soon look like a welcoming oasis, especially from the air.

Junipers provide safe nesting for birds like this yellow-billed cuckoo.

Go Casual

While most gardeners strive for neatness, birds are partial to messy surroundings, so birdscaping focuses on finding a happy medium—a natural look that will coax birds into lingering and possibly even nesting. Let your perennials, shrubs and other plants knit together, instead of keeping bare space around every plant. Allow the dead leaves to lie beneath shrubs and hedges as an insect-rich mulch for gray catbirds, thrashers, wrens and other friends to investigate.

Hold off on cutting back flower beds until spring so goldfinches, titmice, doves, quail and other birds can shelter in them when searching for seeds and insects in winter. Instead of getting out the clippers every few months to trim, learn to love the natural look of a free-form hedge.

Birds will appreciate it. And you'll appreciate the birds bringing life to your yard, every season of the year.

Calling All Birds

Like any successful recipe, attracting more birds to your backyard requires the right ingredients. The basics are food, water, cover and safe places to raise young. Here's a list of plants and other items that will help you succeed:

Fruit-, nut- or seed-bearing trees and shrubs

Golden King holly with berries

- Cherry
- Crabapple
- Dogwood
- Hawthorn
- Highbush cranberry
- Holly
- Mountain ash
- Mulberry
- Raspberry
- Red cedar (Juniper)
- Serviceberry
- Sumac

Shrubs and conifers for shelter, protective cover and nesting areas

- Fir
- Hemlock
- Juniper
- Manzanita
- Mesquite
- Rhododendron
- Pine
- Spruce

Rhododendron fastigiatum

Perennials and annuals that provide seeds and nectar sources

Purple coneflower

- Asters
- Bee balm
- Coreopsis
- Cosmos
- Goldenrod
- Joe-pye weed
- Marigold
- Purple coneflower
- Red-hot poker
- Salvia
- Sedum
- Sunflower
- Zinnia

Vines for cover and nest sites

- American bittersweet
- Clematis
- Grape
- Honeysuckle
- Trumpet vine

Suet and sugar water

- Ground feeders
- Hanging feeders
- Post-mounted feeders
- Tabletop or tray feeders

More backyard features to attract birds

- Birdbaths for bathing and drinking
- Birdhouses for cavity-nesting birds
- Brush piles for shelter, nesting and protection

fruit for birds

Bring in an array of new visitors just by serving up oranges, bananas and more.

BY SALLY ROTH

If you offer only one fruit, you can't go wrong with oranges. They can attract more than 10 species, including orioles.

It's easy to bring a whole rainbow of birds to your yard by simply expanding your spring menu. Add an offering of fruit to your seeds and suet, and you're likely to attract ruby-red tanagers, bright orange orioles, yellow-splotched warblers, green-hued vireos, blue buntings, purple finches and more. (We weren't kidding about the rainbow.) It can't be just any fruit, though. The secret is serving fruits these birds already recognize.

Feasting on Sweets

Birds that migrate for the winter, like tanagers, rose-breasted grosbeaks, orioles, thrashers and wrens, are accustomed to having fruit free for the pecking, available every day on their wintering grounds and at many stops on the way back.

When tanagers, orioles and other friends depart from their winter paradise in spring to head back to nesting grounds in North America, they can stop off in Brazil for bananas, then munch on mangoes in Ecuador and grab a bite of citrus in Nicaragua or Florida. (Not to mention the myriad other tropical fruits we don't even recognize, such as soursop, sapote, sapodilla and dragon fruit.)

Eventually, usually by late April to May, our feathered fliers hit the colder parts of their route, where fruit season is still many weeks away. Luckily, the burgeoning hatch of insects fills the gap on the last leg of the long journey. And so does fruit at feeders.

Best Feeder Fruits

In spring, migrants are looking for sweet, fresh, juicy fruits. Just a few weeks ago they were pecking at oranges, bananas and other prizes right on the tree, and that's what will get their attention in a hurry. Try these guaranteed-to-please offerings at your feeder, and enjoy the rainbow of eager eaters that may soon come calling.

ORANGES. A cheap, ordinary orange is the quickest and easiest way to grab the attention of fruit-loving spring migrants. Orioles are likely to be the first arrivals, and you may also see tanagers, grosbeaks of at least

Western tanager

three species (rose-breasted, blue or black-headed), northern parula and other wood warblers, thrashers and other eye-catching friends pecking at the fruit. The same migrants that love oranges readily accept grapefruit. Tangerines, clementines and even lemons also find takers.

BANANAS. Hang a small bunch of partly peeled bananas from a metal shepherd's hook, or set a peeled banana in an open tray feeder. Then watch for the scarlet tanagers, summer tanagers, hepatic tanagers, orioles of every description, vireos, wood warblers, buntings, gray catbirds, thrashers and others that will soon discover it.

PEARS. A ripe, juicy pear is a prime target for lazuli, indigo and painted buntings, all species of tanagers and orioles, wrens, rose-breasted and black-headed grosbeaks, purple finches and other spring migrants that love fruit. Even flickers and other woodpeckers may be tempted.

PEACHES. Purple finches, house finches and Cassin's finches are special fans of fresh, sweet peaches. In commercial or backyard orchards, these birds can become pests because each bird takes only a few bites of each peach, ruining the crop. When only one peach is available at the feeder, though, they usually eat every bit.

Lasting Effects

Birds have good memories. They know where they found a bounty of food before, and they'll return just as reliably as your hummingbirds do to their nectar feeder.

If the habitat suits their needs, tanagers, orioles, bluebirds and other feeder visitors may even choose your yard or a nearby spot to raise their family. A reliable source of desirable food is a strong incentive when it's time to find a nest site.

So add one or more kinds of fruit to your feeder and yard, and you're sure to enjoy a spectrum of winged friends for years to come.

a sure sign of summer

Learn how to bring ducks closer, and enjoy their playful ways all season.

BY **DAVID MIZEJEWSKI**

It's just not summer without ducks waddling about. With their chatty quacking, large size, beautiful plumage and adorable young, they're some of the most entertaining wildlife to watch. They attract even more attention in summer when the little ones are all lined up behind their mother, crossing the road or on their way to the pond.

They might not be traditional songbirds, but they're still a backyard favorite. Here's a glimpse of this fun bird family.

Learning the Basics

Ducks eat a mix of plant and animal matter, depending on the species and time of year. Dabbling ducks filter

When called by their mother, wood duck young jump from their nest within a day of hatching.

aquatic plants, insects, crustaceans, and tiny fish and amphibians (and their eggs) from shallow waters. Diving ducks hunt fish beneath the surface. On land, some ducks feed on berries, seeds, nuts, foliage, snails, insects and amphibians.

Ducks are some of the fastest and strongest fliers in the sky. They're no slouches on the ground, either; I once saw a duck pluck a lightning-fast dragonfly right out of the air as it flew by her head.

When it comes to providing habitat for ducks, it's all about one thing: They depend on sizable bodies of water for both foraging and protection from land-based predators. A birdbath or even a small water garden will obviously not suffice. If you have the space and your zoning laws allow it, you could excavate a larger pond that will surely appeal to ducks. If you're lucky enough to live near a lake or slow-moving river, these birds probably already visit.

Attracting Ducks

The best way to make ducks feel at home is to plant a wide variety of native plants and to stop using both pesticides and fertilizers. Native plants along the shoreline offer food sources, nesting places and cover from predators, especially for the young. Pesticides will kill insects that ducks feed on and possibly harm fish and amphibians as well—which are not only important wildlife but food sources. Residential fertilizer runoff is one of the biggest sources of water pollution, which destroys waterfowl habitat on a grand scale.

You can entice some duck species to nest in your yard. Common ground-nesting ducks such as mallards will take advantage of a nesting platform strategically hidden in the shoreline vegetation—or better yet, floating away from the shore. Wood ducks are cavity nesters and will use nesting boxes placed over the water.

Whether they're in your backyard or not, I hope you have the chance to observe ducks this summer. Once you start watching these distinctive birds, it's hard to stop.

room *for* rent

Discover which cavity dwellers you can attract to your backyard.

BY KENN AND KIMBERLY KAUFMAN

Carolina wrens are among the easiest birds to attract to a backyard birdhouse.

For parent birds, raising a nest full of babies can be a risky project. With predators around every corner, many parents hide their nests among dense foliage or in tall grass for protection. Another approach is to put it inside a tree. This cavity-nesting strategy is practiced by all kinds of birds, including some that you can attract to your backyard.

The Builders

Left alone, a mature tree may develop cavities in spots where branches have fallen off or large limbs have decayed from within. But some birds don't wait around for these cavities to develop naturally—they make their own.

Members of the woodpecker family are expert homebuilders. They usually excavate their own nest holes, choosing spots in dead trees or limbs. They're quite industrious about it, too. Typically, a pair of woodpeckers will dig a new nest hole for each new brood that they raise. In fall, they also dig holes to roost in during winter. Because they tend to keep excavating new holes instead of reusing old ones, they leave behind ready-made nest sites for many other birds.

Fix-Up Artists

Most birds don't have the chisel-shaped bills of woodpeckers, so they aren't so well-equipped for excavating in dead wood. But some cavity nesters are willing to enlarge or modify existing small holes, and sometimes create their own.

Chickadees, with their tiny bills, don't look as if they could create their own nest cavities, but they often do, enlarging a small knothole or digging a complete hole in soft, decaying wood. Nuthatches may modify existing holes or dig new ones. The oak titmouse on the West Coast will alter holes to suit its needs, but its eastern cousin, the tufted titmouse, seems to simply use holes as it finds them.

Popular Tenants

A standard birdhouse, or nest box, is simply an artificial version of a natural tree cavity. Several popular birds have adapted to nest boxes,

Red-breasted sapsuckers, as well as other sapsuckers and woodpeckers, excavate cavities, which are reused by many kinds of birds.

WREN: MASLOWSKI WILDLIFE/VISUALS UNLIMITED/GETTY IMAGES; SAPSUCKER: MARIE READ

Prothonotary warblers are one of the few warblers that will use a nest box.

giving backyard birders abundant opportunities for up-close views. Bluebirds are found all across the continent, and all three species—eastern, western and mountain—raise their young either in natural cavities or in nest boxes. The bluebird's popularity has been a bonanza for the tree swallow, another cavity nester, which uses holes of the same size.

The purple martin is another classic birdhouse species in eastern North America. Practically all martins east of the Rockies now nest in multiroomed martin houses, sometimes with dozens of pairs sharing space in the same structure. In the West, some martins still nest in the traditional way, in cavities in dead trees—or, in the Arizona desert, in holes in giant cactus.

The High-Wren District

Wrens are mostly shades of brown and gray, but they make up for their lack of bright colors with high-energy personalities and musical songs. Five species—about half our wrens—are cavity nesters. The house wren is widespread from coast to coast, while the Bewick's wren lives mainly in the West, and the Carolina wren is most common in the Southeast. The tiny winter wren nests in the Northwoods,

5 TIPS FOR APPEALING TO CAVITY DWELLERS

1. Leave dead wood standing where you can. Of course, some dead trees and dead limbs have to come down for safety's sake. But if they won't fall on people or property, standing pieces of dead wood can be magnets for woodpeckers, which dig nest cavities and then leave them for other birds to use.

2. Consider "planting" a dead tree. Kimberly once hauled in a couple of huge cottonwood logs, dug 6-foot holes and "planted"

the logs upright at the back of her yard. Within a couple of years, she had woodpeckers, chickadees, wrens and other birds nesting.

3. Go easy on the pesticides. There are exceptions, but most cavity-nesting birds are insect-eaters. If you use poisons to kill insects in your yard, the birds may not have enough to eat.

4. Put up nest boxes. No dead trees around? You can still attract many cavity nesters by putting up boxes for them. It's best to

plan for specific types of birds rather than putting up generic birdhouses that might not be appropriate.

5. Don't encourage competitors for nest sites. Nonnative birds such as house sparrows and European starlings often take over nest cavities from our native birds. If sparrows and starlings mob your bird feeders, it might be wise to stop feeding during nesting season.

while its close relative, the Pacific wren, resides in the Far West.

These birds loosely define a "cavity" for nesting. They will nest in standard tree holes or nest boxes, but they also use crevices in buildings, hollows among the roots of fallen trees, old flowerpots in sheds—just about any enclosed space. House wrens have even been found building nests in the pockets of trousers hanging on clotheslines!

Surprising Cavity Nesters

Several other types of birds are also among the cavity crew. Various kinds of owls nest in cavities, including little screech-owls, which may lurk unnoticed in holes even in suburban backyards. The American kestrel, a colorful little falcon, uses tree holes or nest boxes in open country. Flashy wood ducks adopt tree hollows or nest boxes close to the water; hooded mergansers, common goldeneyes and buffleheads are among the other cavity-nesting waterfowl.

Those are all fairly large birds, but our last two examples are tiny. Of the 55 species of warblers in North America, only two nest in cavities: Lucy's warbler, a pale gray bird of southwestern deserts, and the prothonotary warbler, a brilliant golden sprite of southeastern swamps. They remind us that nature is full of surprises. They also remind us that, regardless of what your dentist might say, cavities can be good things!

If you live near water, be sure to put out a house for wood ducks.

Don't forget to look for owls nesting in tree cavities, like this pygmy owl.

Swainson's thrush

FALL PLANTS
for birds

*Provide an autumn feast and ample
shelter for your visitors.*

BY DAVID MIZEJEWSKI

You know the fall routine: Deciduous
woody trees and shrubs as well as
herbaceous perennials and grasses
go dormant, losing foliage, shutting
down active photosynthesis and
transpiration. Evergreens slow down,
too. But planting in the fall months
means that new additions to the
garden are less likely to experience
transplant shock and die, and that's
good for you as well as for the birds
you're trying to attract.

As you choose your new plantings,
make sure to include species that
provide the two main elements of
habitat that birds require in the fall:
food and shelter.

In early fall, insects are still
plentiful and make up a portion of
most birds' diets. But as the days grow

When buying new plants, do some research first and take the botanical name with you to the nursery to ensure that you're getting exactly what you want.

American robin in a flowering dogwood tree

Look for These Fall Fruit Eaters

Robins	Wild turkeys
Catbirds	Finches
Thrushes	Wood ducks
Bluebirds	Orioles
Tanagers	Chickadees
Grosbeaks	Thrashers
Waxwings	Crossbills
Woodpeckers	Mockingbirds
Jays	Tree swallows

shorter and the weather colder, insects die off or go dormant. Just as bears preparing for hibernation fatten up on berries and nuts, birds, too, look to these food sources in fall.

Migratory birds in particular seek out fruiting plants in early fall as they head to their wintering grounds. They burn massive numbers of calories as they embark on their long migrations and need to regularly stop and eat along the way. The best source of fall food is fruiting shrubs and small trees, and the best way to attract migrants is to include them in your yard.

Dogwood fruits are especially important this time of year; they ripen just about the same time birds begin their fall migration. This is no coincidence. Dogwood fruit is high

in fat, which is an excellent energy source to fuel strenuous migration. The dogwoods benefit by having their seeds spread by the birds. Flowering, redtwig and gray dogwoods are particularly good food sources in early fall. So are elderberry, native viburnums (including arrowwood, nannyberry and mapleleaf), white oaks, crabapple and even wild grapes.

Nonmigratory resident bird species are also on the lookout for fruits during the fall and will join their migratory counterparts to feed at early-fruiting plants. These birds will be sticking around once the migrants have all departed, so make sure that you have plenty of plants that hold their fruit through the season. Some good choices are chokeberry, bayberry,

American cranberry bush, sumacs, hawthorns and winterberry holly.

Don't forget the evergreens, which serve another autumn need: shelter. Evergreens are perfect places for birds to get out of the wet and cold, as well as to hide from hungry predators. Plant whatever pines, spruces, junipers or cedars are native to your area. Eastern redcedar (actually a juniper) and spruce trees also produce cones that birds relish in fall.

Add a birdbath to boot, and you'll have the perfect seasonal oasis for birds in autumn!

sunny-side up

Brighten your backyard and lure birds with sunflowers.

BY KRIS WETHERBEE

10 terrific sunflower varieties, from pint-sized plants to true giants, that will help you entice birds.

1. AUTUMN BEAUTY: Multibranching plant grows about 5 feet tall, with single and bicolor blooms up to 8 inches across in yellow, bronze and purple.

2. BIG SMILE: Dwarf, extra-early variety from 1 to 2 feet tall with bright, golden-yellow blooms up to 6 inches across.

3. FLORISTAN: Multibranching plant grows 3 to 4 feet tall, with bicolor blooms of reddish-brown tipped in yellow.

4. HOLIDAY: Multibranching, 6-foot-tall plant with 3- to 5-inch golden-yellow flowers that surround brown centers.

5. THE JOKER: Beautiful fully double, semidouble or single 4- to 5-inch flowers in a two-tone mix of mahogany and golden-yellow on 6-foot-tall plants. This is a pollen-free variety, which means you don't have to worry about getting pollen on the table when you use it as a cut flower.

6. RUSSIAN GIANT: This type grows to 12 feet tall with large 12- to 14-inch heads and a bounty of edible seeds that people and birds can enjoy.

7. RED SUN: Multibranching plant grows to 6 feet tall with up to 10 6-inch blooms per plant, each with dark centers surrounded by bronze-red petals with orange-red tips.

8. SORAYA: All-America Selections winner in 2000; boasts single orange-tinted flowers, 4 to 6 inches across. It grows 5 to 6 feet tall.

9. VALENTINE: Bold plant to 5 feet tall with a profusion of lemon-yellow flowers 4 to 6 inches across with chocolate-brown centers; good as a long-lasting cut flower.

10. VANILLA ICE: Multibranched plant with creamy-colored blooms and dark centers that grows 4 to 7 feet tall.

Sunflowers are one of the great American gardening traditions. These cheery sun worshipers have broad appeal, not only for the beauty they bring to any outdoor space, but also for the bounty of birds and butterflies they attract with sweet nectar and high-energy seeds.

Sunflower seeds attract a wider variety of birds than any other type of feeder seed. If these power-packed seeds can make your bird feeding stations a favorite destination spot, just imagine what they can do when growing in your garden!

The sunflower family *(Helianthus)* includes about 70 different summer- and autumn-blooming annuals and perennials, though this native American plant is best known for the common or giant sunflower *(Helianthus annuus)*.

America's love affair with sunflowers is changing—not in the ways we enjoy them, but rather in the kinds we grow. A new generation of botanical beauties offers more variety than ever before.

Compact varieties grow just 1 to 4 feet tall and work well in container gardens, in a children's garden or as border or edging plants. Taller, multibranching types grow 4 to 6 feet tall and produce more flowers per plant, providing a bird buffet with even more appeal. These multibranched varieties are outstanding when mingled in flower beds and borders, as focal points in the vegetable garden or even arranged in semicircles as "sunflower forts" for kids.

Consider selecting more than just one variety or even one plant. Growing several varieties with different forms, colors and heights amplifies the visual interest in your garden—as well as the visual attraction to butterflies and birds.

And because sunflowers rely on cross-pollination, they require two or more plants to yield ample seeds. More plants mean more flowers for you and more seeds for the birds. What could be better than that?

Grow Plants for Birds
Readers swear by these plant picks for attracting birds.

1

I plant sunflowers, Mexican sunflowers and zinnias to attract hummingbirds and other beautiful birds. Making sure to have plenty of water for them also helps.
Ella Lucas
ROANOKE, VIRGINIA

2

Attract tons of birds by creating a mini bird haven in an unused corner of your yard. I planted viburnum, ornamental grasses and purple coneflowers. Then I added a shepherd's hook with feeders.
Barbara Manheim
NEW LENOX, ILLINOIS

3

I've discovered that Montana bluets and zinnias provide food for American goldfinches. The birds bend the drying flower heads to the ground as they land on them, then pull out the seeds with their bills.
Charlene Margetiak
NORWALK, OHIO

4

Plant mountain ash, noninvasive honeysuckle, crabapple trees and a Juneberry tree to attract the birds. Inviting birds to your backyard with these plants will help control the bug population, too.
Azalea Wright
FOREST LAKE, MINNESOTA

5

Daylilies not only fill your yard with dazzling colors, but they also attract nectar-feeding birds like hummingbirds and orioles.
Marlene Condon
CROZET, VIRGINIA

breathtaking Blooms

Fill your yard with perennials, annuals, shrubs and trees that burst with brilliant color. Create gorgeous containers to instantly brighten any space. Change up your landscape with a unique rock or rain garden.

MARTIN RUEGNER/GETTY IMAGES

top 10 classic yellows

Flowers in this sunny hue are guaranteed to add some garden drama.

BY KIRSTEN SWEET

1

They say if you have a yellow personality type, you're cheerful, friendly and fun to be around. I'd say the same is true of yellow flowers, wouldn't you? You can find yellow blooms for a wide range of garden styles, from high-impact modern landscapes to romantic cottage flower beds. Consider these 10 yellow picks, sure to be a welcome addition to your space.

1 Sunflower

Helianthus annuus, annual

Show off your love of yellow on a new level—literally. Sunflowers can grow over 15 feet tall. And as you can imagine, they love a good, hot summer. Attractive to bees and birds, sunflowers shine if you're looking for an easy way to lure wildlife to your backyard.

TRY THIS: For a spin on the classic shape, choose the compact Teddy Bear variety. The 6-inch double blooms are real showstoppers in borders, bouquets or containers.

2 Blanket flower

Gaillardia x grandiflora, Zones 3 to 10

This short-lived perennial blooms best in full sun and well-draining soil. The 3-inch blooms attract butterflies and the plant will grow to be about 18 inches tall.

TRY THIS: The Mesa Yellow blanket flower is great for stunning blossoms with brilliant petals and matching centers. Unlike many other blanket flower varieties, it offers loads of flowers and a uniform habit.

3 Daffodil

Narcissus, Zones 3 to 8

Daffodils' sunny trumpets are among the first beacons of spring. They'll grow in most types of soil and don't mind some shade. Keep daffodils in mind as summer winds down, because you'll need to plant them in autumn. They're also pretty resilient, growing in woodlands, between shrubs and even in rock gardens.

TRY THIS: February Gold is an extra-early bloomer. The long middle trumpet sets it apart from other daffodils.

4 Goldenrod

Solidago, Zones 4 to 9

Known for its small yellow elongated flower heads, goldenrod grows along roadsides, riverbanks and in prairies. A late bloomer, it's ideal for planting in a late-summer border or native garden. Reaching up to 3 feet high, this charming eye-catcher combines well with ornamental grasses.

TRY THIS: Goldrush goldenrod is a butterfly favorite, with masses of yellow flowers that nearly conceal the pretty green foliage.

4

5 Rose

Rosa spp., Zones 2 to 9

The well-loved rose has been cultivated for many centuries. The best part about it? It's available in hundreds of cultivars, with varying habits and flower forms. As a rule of thumb, give roses a sunny spot for optimal flowering.

TRY THIS: Golden Celebration is a pretty yellow selection with dense ruffled petals and a sweet, fruity scent.

6 Ligularia

Ligularia, Zones 4 to 8

These golden flower spikes, reaching about 4 feet tall, love moisture and will add quite a bit of interest if planted near a backyard pond or stream. If you don't have water, ligularia prefers sun and reliably moist soil.

TRY THIS: Surrounded by a clump of dense foliage, Bottle Rocket ligularia's flowering stems shoot straight up, showing off the mustard yellow blooms.

7 Black-Eyed Susan Vine

Thunbergia alata, annual

This vibrant vine shows off its angled petals in summertime. Its spindly stems grow up to 8 feet long, but don't worry about this one getting out of control. Even though it's a vine, you can count on it to stay in bounds.

TRY THIS: Climbing up a trellis or spilling over an arbor, Sunny Lemon Star makes a bold statement.

5

6

7

8 Snapdragon

Antirrhinum majus, annual

Though it usually blooms for most of the growing season, this distinctive flower's spikes put on the display in cooler weather. Deadheading is required to prolong growing, and you'll want to do it—because everyone knows that snapdragon blooms are fun to snap open like puppets.

TRY THIS: We especially like the lacy Rocket Lemon hybrid, which grows about 3 feet tall—perfect for popping up from the back of the flower bed.

9 Tickseed

Coreopsis, Zones 3 to 10

Always a garden favorite, coreopsis is a stunning yellow pick. Plant it in well-drained soil in full sun or partial shade for best results. It also makes a beautiful cut flower, so keep it in mind when you'd like a fresh bouquet.

TRY THIS: With distinctive fluted petals, Jethro Tull is a long and prolific bloomer. Its compact habit makes it a natural for the front of a flower bed.

10 Coneflower

Echinacea, Zones 2 to 9

Gone are the days when all coneflowers were purple. *Echinacea* has burst onto the scene in yellow, pink, white and even green. It's an easy-care, sun-loving favorite, varying in height from 2 to 5 feet. Encourage more compact growth by pruning coneflowers early in the season.

TRY THIS: The 3-inch Cleopatra coneflower, shining in bright yellow, sits atop strong stems. As they age, the blooms fade to an appealing creamy yellow.

Using yellow in the garden

So you've decided to plant yellow flowers. Now you have to figure out what to plant next to your bright, cheery blooms. Yellow is opposite purple on the color wheel, making the two a natural complementary pair. Try planting purple hydrangea next to your tickseed, or climbing clematis behind your snapdragon. Or give salvia a spot near your yellow rose bushes. The possibilities are endless!

top 10 flowers for a cutting garden

Plant these blooms with indoor bouquets in mind.

BY KIRSTEN SWEET

1

I recently became accustomed to having fresh flowers on my dining room table. It started off as a little treat now and then, but I kept feeling as if something was missing whenever my favorite green vase was bare. Ten dollars at the farmers market here and $14 at the grocery store there can really add up.

My solution for a constant (and expensive!) desire for fresh blossoms indoors? A cutting garden! It's so obvious now that I'm kicking myself for not thinking of it sooner. I'm telling you about it now so you can get your plans in the works for your very own cutting garden this year. I chose 10 of my favorites to complete this list, but grow what you like and enjoy fresh bouquets in your house all summer.

1 Speedwell

Veronica spp., Zones 3 to 9

If you want to make a big impact, put several spikes of Veronica speedwell together right in the middle of your flower arrangement. They'll add height and interest. Look for long-blooming varieties.

WHY WE LOVE IT: I'm a sucker for the drama of Veronica speedwell. Those beautiful spikes are major eye-catchers that come in white, purple, pink or blue. They'll bloom for a long time both inside and outside, but trust me: You'll want to bring them in.

2 Stock

Matthiola, annual

Also called garden stock and gillyflower, the blooms of stock grow tall and as a tight cluster. The flower clusters might make the plant a little heavy, so you may need to stake it in the garden. Cut stock when about two-thirds of the blooms are open and it should do well in a vase.

WHY WE LOVE IT: The best part about including stock in your flower arrangement is the sweet and spicy scent. Some say it smells like cloves.

3 Bachelor's buttons

Centaurea cyanus, annual

You might know this beauty as cornflower. And if you're familiar with it, you probably love how easy it is to grow. They are prolific growers that require very little care but offer many rewards. Bachelor's buttons make pretty dried flowers, too!

WHY WE LOVE IT: Bachelor's buttons are beautiful and long-lasting as cut flowers. Their large variety of lively colors will add brightness to any arrangement. Look for them in blue, pink, red, white and purple.

4 Cosmos

Cosmos spp., annual

Cosmos is a garden favorite that is known to attract birds and butterflies, but you don't want to give this one completely to your winged friends. Cut cosmos and take it inside and enjoy it yourself.

WHY WE LOVE IT: If it's versatility you're after, cosmos is it. Tons of varieties and colors are available. Find one that will complement the rest of the blooms in your cutting garden.

5 Shasta daisy

Leucanthemum x superbum, Zones 4 to 9

You can't beat the classic daisy look of a Shasta daisy! It's a strong grower with sturdy stems and a long vase life, making it an ideal cut flower. It'll also look delightful in containers or flower beds. Northern gardeners should divide Shasta daisies every year or so for the longevity of the plant.

WHY WE LOVE IT: I love floral arrangements that include Shasta daisies because the white provides a calm among all the crazy colors of the other blooms I enjoy. And it'll probably be one of the last standing in your bouquet.

6 Globe amaranth

Gomphrena globosa, annual

It's hard not to like globe amaranth. It's a prolific bloomer that will last until frost. And in general, this plant isn't fussy. It'll tolerate various soils and moisture levels—basically a gardener's dream.

WHY WE LOVE IT: The round blooms of globe amaranth add that fun element to an arrangement that not many flowers can. I personally love the globe look and the bright colors! Look for it in pink, purple and white.

7 Peony

Paeonia, Zones 3 to 9

They say it's best to cut peonies in the morning. You'll get a better vase life out of them if you cut them when they're not fully open. But before you bring them in, beware of little bugs or ants that might be hiding in the blossoms.

WHY WE LOVE IT: I love peonies for their large, full blooms. Peonies have a small window in spring when they can be used as a cut flower, so even just a few peonies alone can make a gorgeous small bouquet.

8 Astilbe

Astilbe spp., Zones 4 to 9

A shade favorite, astilbe offers a vertical softness to the garden, and the leaves have a fernlike appearance. After harvesting, put astilbe in water right away. Letting the stems dry out for even a short time will drastically reduce its life as a cut flower.

WHY WE LOVE IT: I love different heights and textures in my bouquets, so that's why astilbe is on my list. Cut them just before you're going to prepare your bouquet and when the blooms are half open.

9 Sunflower

Helianthus annuus, annual

Don't worry; you don't need to bring a sunflower the size of your head indoors. There are dwarf varieties that work perfectly as a cut flower. Harvest sunflowers once their petals have arched upward. Make sure there's water close—you'll want to stick the stems in water right away.

WHY WE LOVE IT: The best feature of sunflowers is the many varieties available. Each one will add something distinct to both your bouquet and outdoor garden by way of different sizes and colors.

10 Bells of Ireland

Moluccella laevis, annual

I'm new to bells of Ireland, but I can't get enough. This heirloom has pale-lime leaves, which accent the green whorls that look like blooms. The flowers are actually inside the cuplike whorls. Bells of Ireland are easy to grow from seed and you can effortlessly transport them to a vase.

WHY WE LOVE IT: My reason for loving this is simple: It's just a cool-looking plant. It'll add some green pizzazz to a cut flower arrangement.

6 TIPS FOR A BETTER BOUQUET

1. **GO INTO THE GARDEN EARLY.** Cut flowers in the morning. Take a bucket with you to the flower bed so you can immediately put the stems in water.

2. **PAY ATTENTION TO BLOOM COUNT AND MATURITY.** When cutting blossoms from the garden, choose flowers that are at various stages of blooming. That way, you can enjoy seeing new buds open indoors.

3. **PREVENT DROOPING.** As you place the flowers in the vase, crisscross the stems. This will give them a solid base and help them stay in place.

4. **FILL IN THE GAPS.** Filler plants like lady's mantle, fennel, ornamental grasses or even hostas are pleasing additions that can fill in any bare spots.

5. **DON'T OVERTHINK IT.** You could spend all day arranging and rearranging the flowers in a bouquet. They'll be beautiful no matter how you place them.

6. **CHANGE THE WATER FREQUENTLY.** Most fresh-cut flowers will benefit from clean water every day.

10
black plants

The new black is just black when it comes to the world of horticulture. Check out some of our favorites.

BY STACY TORNIO

1

When I first heard about black plants, I wondered what the fuss was about. Plants and flowers are supposed to be bright and colorful. Why would anyone want dark and dreary?

But then I saw my first black petunia—wow! I couldn't believe how gorgeous and captivating it was. My newfound love didn't stop with petunias. Once I started looking, I began noticing many cool plants with dark, rich foliage and blooms. While some were more like black wannabes, falling into the purple or brown section of the color wheel, I was still impressed with the selection. Take a look at some of my favorites, but be sure to do a little exploring on your own as well. After all, I hear every garden looks good in black.

1 Zwartkop aeonium

Aeonium arboreum, Zones 9 to 11

It's hard to find a more dramatic and impressive black plant than this black rose aeonium. This succulent does best in at least a half day of full sun. If grown in more shade, the rosettes are reddish-purple with a green center. It grows up to 12 inches tall and tolerates drought and poor soil. If you live out of Zone 9 to 11 (and let's face it, you probably do), then overwinter it indoors!

WHY WE LOVE IT: Though it looks stunning with some bright-yellow petunias or pansies, we think it makes a statement all on its own.

2 Midnight Ruffles hellebore

Helleborus, Zones 4 to 9

This double-bloom hellebore actually has three times as many petals as a single-bloom hellebore. Combine that with its amazing velvety flowers, and it's easy to see why this plant has the horticulture world talking. It grows nearly 24 inches tall and wide, and is ideal for shade.

WHY WE LOVE IT: It's an early bloomer! Hellebores start flowering in late winter and continue for several weeks. In fact, it's also known as Lenten rose, because some varieties bloom during Lent.

3 Tropicanna Black canna

Canna, Zones 7 to 11

Boasting bright scarlet blooms, the Tropicanna Black series offers a refreshing alternative for cannas. You'll need to plant the rhizomes every spring. Then sit back and watch the magic as they grow up to 6 feet tall. The plants do best with at least six hours of sun, but will tolerate some shade.

WHY WE LOVE IT: It's one of the easiest ways to bring the flair of the tropics to your backyard.

4 Black Velvet petunia

Petunia x hybrid, annual

Are you ready for the world's first black petunia? Here it is! Ball Horticulture Co. introduced Black Velvet a few years ago. A perfect fit for containers, it thrives in sunny areas.

WHY WE LOVE IT: Containers just got more interesting, thanks to the richness of this plant. Pair it with bright-pink blooms for a lively contrast.

5 Sorbet Black Delight viola

Viola cornuta, annual

Also known as horned violet, the low-maintenance, fragrant viola tolerates sun and partial shade and blooms most profusely in cool weather. Everyone should grow some violas, so why not try this bold cultivar?

WHY WE LOVE IT: You know how you get that itch to garden even before the chance of frost has passed? Grow this viola—it's forgiving.

6 Black Coral elephant ear

Colocasia esculenta, Zones 7 to 10

Elephant ear is a plant that already commands attention with its giant leaves. This black-leafed variety is even more striking, growing nearly 4 feet tall with leaves 3 feet or more across! Even if you live in a colder zone, you can enjoy this beauty year after year. Just dig it up and keep it in a cool place over winter.

WHY WE LOVE IT: It's one of the most distinctive plants for containers, but you're going to need a big one! Plant it as the centerpiece and accent with bright plants around it.

7 Black Prince coleus

Coleus solenostemon, annual

You'll have plenty of versatility with this tough coleus—it does well in sun or shade and is perfect for container combinations, hanging baskets or garden beds. (You can even grow it as a houseplant.) It grows to about 30 inches tall and will attract hummingbirds with its late-season flowers.

WHY WE LOVE IT: It's very forgiving if you sometimes forget to water it. If you see it start to droop, just add water and it'll perk right up.

5, 6, 9, 10, HOLLYHOCK: PERENNIALRESOURCE.COM; 7: PROVENWINNERS.COM; 8: JOHN GLOVER/ALAMY

8 Victoriana Silver Lace Black primrose

Primula elatior, Zones 5 to 10

As winter turns to spring, little blooms appear on these compact dark-green plants. Victoriana Silver Lace Black boasts white-edged petals and a golden-yellow center. The primrose does best in partial shade, but it can live in full sun if the soil around it remains moist.

WHY WE LOVE IT: The pattern! The standout colors remind us of a kaleidoscope.

9 Before the Storm tall bearded iris

Iris, Zones 3 to 10

Irises are a staple in backyard gardens, and they're available in just about every shade imaginable, including this new purplish-black variety. This one has a bit of a sweet fragrance and blooms in early summer, making it the perfect plant to provide garden color in the lull between tulips and flowering perennials. Like all tall bearded irises, it performs best in full sun.

WHY WE LOVE IT: It's naturally deer- and rabbit-resistant, so if you have trouble with critters eating your plants, give it a try.

10 Obsidian coral bells

Heuchera, Zones 3 to 9

While coral bells do have tiny blooms atop long shoots, many people buy them for the foliage. And why wouldn't you, with options like deep red, orange and black. This Obsidian cultivar is just one of several coral bells with black leaves.

WHY WE LOVE IT: You can plant coral bells in partial shade. And the tiny blooms attract hummingbirds!

Try growing this dark-hued Hollyhock.

More Favorites

Ten ideas not enough? Here are a few more plants to look for:

- Calla lilies (Black Pearl)
- Geranium (Espresso)
- Hollyhock (Blacknight)
- Sweet potato vine (Blackie)
- Bachelor's button (Black Magic)

9

10

Coral bells (also called heuchera) tolerate shady areas and come in an array of colorful foliages.

the bright side of shade

A shade garden isn't doomed to dreary, colorless plant picks. Today's shade choices are more colorful than ever.

BY SALLY ROTH

Just a few years ago, the words "shade garden" brought to mind hostas, ferns, impatiens and maybe some astilbe. Shade gardens were viewed as a fine place to rest awhile on the garden bench, but not nearly as exciting as a sunny border.

Flowers for shade are still more limited than those for sun—especially now that impatiens no longer thrive in many areas due to a fast-spreading fatal disease. But foliage colors have exploded. And oh, the possibilities! Today we can spice up our shade gardens with bright lime, orange, pink, red, burgundy, purple, chocolate, near-black and every shade in between. Foliage plants are no longer considered accents; they are the foundation and the "flowers."

Today's splendid palette lets us use foliage plants as we would blossoms, creating color combinations that last all season. Easy-to-grow coleus, for instance, now comes in an unbelievable selection of luscious colors, with leaves ranging from simple shapes to frilly ruffles, in heights from 8 inches to 3 feet. As a bonus, the flowers also attract hummingbirds.

The tiny flowers of heuchera attract hummers, too, but it's the sumptuous apricot, caramel, rose, lime or plum leaves of the new varieties that steal the show in the garden.

Even ferns have left good old green behind. Take a look at the Lady in Red cultivar, with her lacy fronds and blood-red stems, or silver and burgundy Japanese painted fern, or the autumn fern Brilliance, which starts out coppery pink in spring, turns green for summer, then colors up again for fall.

It's easy to get carried away and come home with one of everything. But instead of throwing them all together, give your fancy plants room to shine beside quieter companions. Remember that serenity is one of the best things about a shade garden. Keep that peaceful feeling by separating different kinds of variegated plants with plainer companions so the leaves aren't fighting each other for the spotlight. Use dark-leaved plants, such as Osiris Café Noir ligularia, Hillside

Black Beauty actaea or Chocoholic cimicifuga, to create "shadows" between your bright-colored beauties so your eyes have a resting place.

Plant a Rainbow

Playing with color is the new shade gardening. Free your fuchsias from the hanging basket and partner them with smoldering red coleus for close-up hummingbird watching. Spice up your summer selection with copper plant (Acalypha wilkesiana), pink Dragon Wings begonia, pink polka-dot plant and red fuchsias.

Add zing to serene green and white hostas and ferns with a pool of blue Summer Wave torenia and an unexpected dash of hot sauce from orange and pink coleus. Mix and match whatever tickles your fancy, combining annuals and perennials with foliage plants that echo or contrast with their colors. For more of our picks for colorful perennials and annuals for shade, be sure to check out the chart on the following page.

Gauge Your Shade

Sure, you can get technical, plotting the arc of the sun and keeping track of how many hours your shady yard gets direct light, in which part of the day, in every season. But if you have a shady part of the yard, you already know it.

Most shade plants do best in part shade or light shade—the usual conditions, even in many forests. Partial shade means a few hours of sun every day; light or dappled shade, created by shifting leaves, may get no direct sun at all, but it gets a good amount of light.

Deep shade is an area where even indirect light rarely penetrates. It's an uncommon situation, but you may have that, too, if you have buildings blocking the sun or other barriers.

Most shade plants are very adaptable when it comes to the degree of shade they prefer. They'll quickly tell you if you've guessed wrong. If they start looking weak and leggy, there's not enough light. If their leaves crisp or curl or start looking bleached

Astilbe comes in colors like white, red and pink.

Columbine

Ligularia

Jacob's ladder

Astilbe

Hellebore

A Rainbow of Color in Shade

PINK
PERENNIAL: Astilbe, bleeding heart, fern-leaf bleeding heart, foxglove, *Geranium cinereum* 'Ballerina', hellebore, winter cyclamen
ANNUAL: Begonias, fuchsia, torenia

RED
PERENNIAL: Astilbe, eastern and western red columbines, fire pink
ANNUAL: Fuchsia, begonias

YELLOW
PERENNIAL: Lamium Hermann's Pride, kirengeshoma, ligularia, wood poppy, woodland sunflower, yellow corydalis
ANNUAL: Monkeyflower, tuberous begonia

GREEN
PERENNIAL: Hellebore
ANNUAL: *Nicotiana langsdorfii*

BLUE/PURPLE
PERENNIAL: Blue wood aster, brunnera, Brookside hardy geranium, Jacob's ladder, liriope, lungwort, monkshood, *Phlox divaricata*, *Phlox stolonifera*, Rocky Mountain columbine, *Scilla siberica*, toad lilies, Virginia bluebells
ANNUAL: Browallia, Summer Wave torenia

WHITE
PERENNIAL: Astilbe, bear's-breeches, Biokovo hardy geranium, hellebore, White Nancy lamium, lily-of-the-valley, snowdrops, tiarella, white wood aster
ANNUAL: Fuchsia, woodland tobacco (*Nicotiana sylvestris*)

Foxglove

Lungwort

MANAGING WITH MAPLES

Shallow roots and a solid canopy of leaves make it tough to garden under maples. For a quick solution, set a group of containers beneath your maple tree, staggering their heights by raising some on upturned pots or bricks. It's much easier to coddle container gardens than to fight the maple roots.

or browned, and you find yourself watering way too much, there's too much sun. Move them, and try something that's better suited to the original spot.

Find Creative Alternatives

Garden centers make it easy by corralling shade plants into separate sections, at least when it comes to perennials, hostas, ferns and annuals. Stroll the shrubs and trees to seek out azaleas and rhododendrons, eastern redbud, dogwood, serviceberry, red-flowering currant, white sweetspire and the shrub Fuchsia magellanica, all good bloomers in shade.

Consider houseplants, too. The filtered natural light in our houses is similar to outdoor shade, and croton, polka dot plant, Moses-in-the-boat, asparagus fern, Swedish ivy and abutilon (flowering maple) will thrive in the ground or in containers for a summer vacation.

Shade gardening is full of exciting possibilities, once you start looking on the bright side. Just think of foliage as beautiful flowers, and you'll have it made in the shade.

Pele coleus

Chocoholic cimicifuga

Ruffles Copper coleus

Obsidian coral bells

bring on the
rain

With a little bit of planning, you can turn rainwater into a hot garden commodity!

BY MELINDA MYERS

Water—it's one of the most essential, beneficial and frustrating assets for gardeners throughout the country. At any given time, there seems to be either too much of it or not enough. So what's the solution? Plant a rain garden!

No, a rain garden won't necessarily solve all your planting problems, but it's one of the most attractive and effective ways to manage inconsistent rainfall in your backyard. The rewards are almost endless: It reduces the risk of flooding and overloading storm sewers, it allows plant roots and soil to filter out impurities before the water goes back into the ground, and it's just plain good for the environment.

While most trees, grasses and other plants naturally help intercept rainwater, rain gardens can soak up as much as 30 percent more water than conventional lawns. If planned right, they also provide a natural habitat for birds, as well as butterflies and other helpful insects. So start planning your rain garden now, and put rainwater to work for you.

Design Is Key

For best results, consider a few things up front. Note your soil type, the slope of the garden area, the distance from the house, the average rainfall for your area and the square footage of hard surfaces such as drives, walks or rooftops where you're collecting water.

You'll want to prepare your garden on a slight slope and at least 10 feet away from your house to avoid water collecting near your foundation. Also, avoid planting rain gardens over septic systems and under trees, where increased soil moisture could cause damage.

If possible, design the garden with the longest end perpendicular to the slope, increasing the border available to intercept water runoff. The garden should be about twice as long as it is wide. This provides plenty of room for plants to help slow down water and absorb it, as well as making it easier for you to come up with an attractive layout for the area.

Do the Dirty Work

Most rain gardens should be 4 to 8 inches deep, but you'll need to take the soil type, slope and size of your garden into account. Make sure the garden is level to avoid water pooling on one side. You may need to move, excavate or add soil to make this happen. It also may help to create a small berm on the garden's downhill edge to help contain water until it can naturally drain.

Dig several inches of compost or other organic matter into the top 6 to 8 inches of soil before planting. This will improve drainage in heavy soils and increase the water retention of fast-draining soils. This step is really crucial, because natural rainfall supplying water to your garden will often be irregular.

A well-designed garden will drain within 12 to 48 hours, avoiding standing water. This is important to the health of your plants and to prevent mosquitoes from breeding in your garden.

Get Planting!

Select plants suited to temporary flooding and drought, since rain gardens are not water gardens, ponds or wetlands. They are designed to capture water during rainfall and quickly drain as plants absorb the moisture and as excess water moves through the garden soil to recharge the groundwater. Ultimately, your goal is to reduce your workload, not increase it.

Begin choosing plants by looking at the native species in your area. Plants native to prairies and swamps or other areas subject to flooding and drought are your best bets, but don't stop there. Also check with nature centers, extension offices and your state department of natural resources to see if they offer regional rain garden suggestions as well.

As you go, use plants with a variety of bloom times for season-long color. Variety is a must. For instance, a mixture of sedges, rushes and other grassy plants makes a dramatic backdrop for flowers.

Place moisture lovers in the lowest areas of the garden that tend to stay wetter longer, and plant drought-tolerant species on the sides or edges of the garden. Once all the plants are in, mulch the garden with twice-shredded bark. This mulch knits together and won't wash away in the rain. Plus, mulching the soil prevents erosion, conserves moisture during dry spells and suppresses weeds. Be careful not to bury the crowns of the plants, though, because that can lead to rot.

Just because you have a rain garden doesn't mean you don't have to water it. Make sure new plantings receive sufficient water, about an inch a week. Adjust the frequency based on the temperature and your soil type. New plantings, even drought-tolerant ones, need regular watering to encourage deep roots that are more efficient at absorbing water.

The Maintenance

Weed regularly the first few years to allow your desirable plants to get established, fill in and outcompete future weeds. Remove dead growth at the start of each season and cut plants back as new growth begins. For an easy spring cleanup, use a string trimmer or mower you can set higher than the new growth. A hand pruner is best for thicker stems like sunflowers, asters and Joe Pye weed.

It's not all work and no play, though. Rain gardens are relatively low maintenance once you get them installed and established. So kick back as you enjoy the birds, butterflies and neighbors that visit your garden. You can feel good about doing your part for the environment, one garden at a time.

Perennials for Rain Gardens

Cardinal flower (*Lobelia cardinalis*)

Black-eyed Susan (*Rudbeckia fulgida*)

Swamp milkweed (*Asclepias incarnata*)

Swamp mallow (*Hibiscus moscheutos*, below)

Joe Pye weed (*Eupatorium*)

Sedges (*Carex*)

Bluestar (*Amsonia*)

Turtlehead (*Chelone*)

If you want an attractive way to slow and direct rainwater, install rain chains!

4 tips for a successful rain garden

1. DO THE RESEARCH AND PLAN. Don't think you can just put in a rain garden on a whim. It takes careful thought and planning.

2. LOCATION DOES MATTER. Make sure your garden is at least 10 feet away from the foundation of your house. Don't plant it under trees, over septic systems or in areas where water might collect.

3. WORK WITH YOUR SOIL. Amend the soil to improve drainage in heavy soils and increase the water retention of porous soils.

4. CHOOSE PLANTS CAREFULLY. Be sure to pick varieties that tolerate both temporary flooding and drought.

Be Water Wise

Don't want to plant a rain garden? Here are some other ideas for conserving water:

- Install rain barrels and cisterns to capture water for use in the landscape.

- Use water from dehumidifiers or air conditioners to water container plants.

- Use drought-tolerant plants.

- Group moisture lovers together.

- Mulch soil to conserve moisture.

breaking tradition

Transplanting isn't just for spring or fall—grab a shovel and dig up those perennials just about anytime.

BY SALLY ROTH

Why didn't I plant those daffodils beside the doorstep? Now I have to wait until fall to transplant!

Daylilies

The best ideas don't always come to us when we want them to. Those coppery orange daylilies in your summer garden, for instance—they sure are showstoppers, but it's a shame the blue veronicas are way over there. They would be glorious with the daylilies.

We've all done it. No matter how much time we spend figuring out where to plant what, we always make mistakes. We think we have it just right—until the plants come into bloom. Then we wish we'd planted those bright Asiatic lilies behind the cool blue campanulas, or partnered the deep red rose with the pure white Shasta daisies, or put the daffodils right beside the doorstep.

It goes on all season, as plants grow and bloom and show us the error of our ways. Sometimes we're off by a matter of inches, or sometimes many feet. Don't live in regret, though. The next time you think, *Why didn't I plant that here instead of there?* just dig right in and fix it on the spot. I call it designing with a shovel.

Playing in the Dirt

Sure, you could wait to transplant misplaced perennials and bulbs until fall, when plants are done blooming, or early spring, when they're just getting growing. But why wait? You can move many perennials—anything with fibrous roots—and just about any bulb while they're in bud or even in bloom.

For best results, transplant on a cloudy day if you can so the plant won't lose moisture to the sun from its leaves. If you can't wait for the weather, transplant in late afternoon. That way the plant can begin settling in without being stressed by a day of sun.

Of course, the most important thing you'll need for designing by shovel is something you already have: water. No matter how careful you are when digging, you're going to slice through some roots, and roots bring the plant water. Until they settle themselves in the new spot, the plant won't be able to get enough water to keep it from wilting. The solution? Watering at every step of the way.

Start by giving the plant you intend to move a good drink so it'll be well-hydrated by the time you transplant. Decide exactly where the plant is going to go. Dig that hole, making it a generous size—about 10 inches across and a shovel-blade deep is a good start. You can adjust it later.

Next, fill the hole with water and let it soak in. Fill it again and let it drain again. If the water still disappears within, say, 20 minutes, do it a third time. The soil should be moist, not muddy; this extra moisture ensures that the surrounding soil won't wick away the water from your transplant.

Time to Get Moving

Now you're ready to begin moving operations. Dig all around the plant (or clump of plants, in the case of bulbs), wider and deeper than you think you need to. For bulbs, dig at least 10 inches deep; for other perennials, you may need to go down only 6 to 8 inches or so. I use a drain spade, sold at hardware stores—its longer, narrower blade is perfect for this operation.

Eyeball the size of the root-ball when you lift it, then gently set the plant back in place. Check your new hole—is it big enough for the roots to fit, and deep enough so the plant will sit at its previous height? If yes, great! If not, adjust the hole. If it's too deep, put some soil back.

"Handle with care" is the motto when transporting the plant. Keep the soil around those roots as intact as you can, and be careful not to break stems or knock off buds. If your plant isn't too big, just carry it on the blade of your shovel to the new hole, supporting it with one hand. For larger plants, use a wheelbarrow. Slide the root-ball into the new hole, and turn the plant until you're satisfied that its best face is forward. Fill the hole halfway with soil and firm it down.

Next, more watering! Fill the hole with water again, but don't wait for it to drain. Go ahead and finish filling in the hole with soil, and pat it down gently so that you don't squish out all the oxygen, because roots need air as much as water. Supply temporary shade for the first day or two to help prevent wilting. An easy way to do this is to set a lawn chair over the plant.

Think of your new transplant as a bouquet of cut flowers for the first week. It needs extra water until those new root hairs take hold, but water too much and you could drown it. If puddles stay on the surface for more than a few minutes, back off with the hose.

It's amazing how quickly a transplant settles in, even if you move it at the peak of bloom. In as little as two to three days, your plant will look as if it's been there forever—in exactly the right place.

Perennial bed with sedum and daylilies

EASY-PEASY

All of these plants, and many more, can be transplanted in bud or bloom: agastache, artemisia, Asiatic lilies, Monch aster, bee balm, bulbs, Goldsturm black-eyed Susan, cardinal flower, campanulas, thread-leaved coreopsis, daylilies, feverfew, liatris, mums, obedient plant, phlox, coneflower, sedum, Shasta daisy, Siberian iris, veronica, yarrow.

Veronica

Black-eyed Susan

Bee balm

gobig

or go home!

When it comes to container gardening, bigger and bolder is always better.

BY STACY TORNIO

If you're going to grow containers,

you might as well *grow containers.* You know, go all out—make a statement—create a living piece of art!

I'm not talking about those little baskets from the garden center filled with the standard petunias, geraniums, impatiens and pansies. Not that there's anything wrong with those—my kids get me a lovely hanging basket of petunias every Mother's Day. But if you're going to invest in good soil, cool pots and unique plants, then you might as well try something distinctive, daring and dramatic. In short, it's time to go big or go home.

1. Find the Right Base

To anchor everything, you need the right container. You'll certainly have plenty of choices. Just go to the garden center, and chances are you'll find rows and rows of them in every size, shape and color imaginable.

Before you even start looking at plants, find a container that inspires you. A short, stocky container would be just the thing for a small conifer. A bold turquoise container would be the perfect backdrop for various shades of pink. A big, tall container is a nice option for trailing plants.

A good pot or other planter can be expensive, but go ahead and splurge a little if you find one you really like. Chances are you'll have it for years. Oh, and remember that containers are like shoes—they're better when you buy them in pairs!

2. Celebrate Height

One of the easiest ways to make an impact with a container is tall plants. Cannas, purple millet and ornamental corn all have big, interesting leaves—and you can't beat the wow factor of a cultivar that's 4 to 6 feet tall.

Another easy way to get height is with ornamental grasses. They not only grow several feet tall in a single season, they also give containers nice texture. You can find some colorful annuals (purple fountain grass, for instance, is an annual in most zones), but don't overlook perennials like switchgrass and zebragrass. Just because you're growing in a container doesn't mean you have to dump the plants out each year. Offer the perennials good protection in a weatherproof pot over the winter, and you'll have a jump on next year.

3. Include Trailing Plants

Trailing plants are a must-have for hanging baskets, but they're also a showstopper for other containers. Garden centers often have a whole section of trailing plants. Use blooms like trailing begonias, petunias and geraniums, or try foliage plants like sweet potato vine and licorice vine.

You'll probably want to stick to a single type of trailing plant per container, but it can be fun to mix in a couple of varieties within a single family. Plant a couple of sweet potato vines, a standard one and a variegated one. They'll complement one another while offering some extra variety.

4. Choose Bold Colors

You don't necessarily want to pair bright red flowers with a bright red container. But with a little bit of planning, you can use color to your advantage. It starts with your pot of choice. How colorful is it? If you love bright orange, yellow or blue pots, what will work well as accents?

Another option is to choose a more subdued, neutral pot that maybe has an interesting shape or lines. Then use plants to make an impact. One advantage to this is that you can change the plants from one year to the next. If you have a brown or terra-cotta pot, you could have a red, white and blue theme one year and a yellow theme the next.

5. The More the Merrier

If you read the label on most cultivars, it's going to say you should space plants 12 to 24 inches apart. But container gardening doesn't abide by those rules. It's better to throw a few extras into the mix, which results in a fuller, bigger, bolder container. Of course, you can go overboard, so use your discretion when planting. If it feels too crowded, it probably is. But if you have lots of soil space, fill it up.

6. Don't Forget About Presentation

So you have your height and your trailing plants. You've chosen an inspiring container. And you've used color to your advantage. Now you just need to make sure that everything works together.

Where will your container live? What do you have planted around it? If it's in a solitary location, is it big enough to fill up the space? The planning and placement of your container are the deciding factors in its success. Give it an outstanding display, and all your hard work will be worthwhile.

container recipes
that make an impact

Here are a few recipes to try out in your backyard.

Orange Surprise
by Ball Horticultural

A New Day™ Clear Orange gazania (2)

B Emerald Falls dichondra (2)

C Silver Falls™ dichondra

D Pony Tails Mexican feather grass

Container size: 14 inches
Exposure: sun

Party of Five
by Proven Winners

A Superbells® Pink calibrachoa

B Northern Lights tufted hairgrass

C Gold Mound duranta

D Lemon Licorice licorice plant

E ColorBlaze® Kingswood Torch coleus

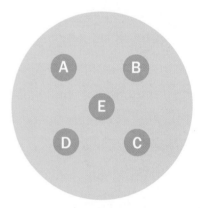

Container size: 24 inches
Exposure: sun

Bands of Gold
by Proven Winners

A Superbells® Red calibrachoa

B GoldDust™ mecardonia

C Amora coleus

Container size: 14 inches
Exposure: sun

Bring happiness to your
backyard by planting these
top picks.

BY CRYSTAL RENNICKE

1

There's nothing quite as welcoming in a winter-weary backyard as a bright sea of tulips ruffling in a spring breeze. Perhaps the most beloved bulbs of all time, tulips come in endless combinations of color, shape and size. And they bloom at so many different times that you can plan to have tulips all season long.

Becky Heath of Brent and Becky's Bulbs (*brentandbeckysbulbs.com*) knows just about every new and old variety on the market. We asked her to help us narrow down our search for the best of the best tulip bulbs. We organized them by category and included bloom time as well. Use this list to help you choose your favorites for planting next fall.

1 Best Lily-flowered: *Ballerina*
Zones 4 to 8

Like long-legged dancers practicing pirouettes, these elegant tulips gracefully sway in the breeze on tall, strong 16- to 20-inch stems. Their sweetly scented petals, with blood-red exteriors and orange-and-yellow edges, may remind you of flickering flames.

WHY WE LOVE IT: It's incredibly hardy, with a lengthy bloom time and striking colors.

BLOOM TIME: Late spring.

2 Best Bicolor: *Prinses Irene*
Zones 3 to 8

Although orange and purple might not be an obvious color combination, this peculiar pairing works perfectly here. The very fragrant, outrageously bright blooms have a pale-purple flame rising up the center. The stately stems grow up to 18 inches tall and look lovely in a bouquet.

WHY WE LOVE IT: We're crazy about odd color pairings, and this one is royally unique. Try it with Jolly Joker pansies, another orange-and-purple beauty.

BLOOM TIME: Early to mid-spring.

3 Best Multiple Flower: *Happy Family*
Zones 3 to 9

Grow happy little tulip families with this fun variety. The petals are purplish-pink and sometimes have a fine white line. This wonderful multiflowering tulip has one large flower, one medium flower and several small blooms: an entire family on one 14- to 16-inch stem!

WHY WE LOVE IT: Gardeners adore getting more bang for their buck, and this tulip reliably grows several blooms per stem.

BLOOM TIME: Mid- to late spring.

4 Best Parrot: *Professor Rontgen*

Zones 4 to 7

Fancy fringed parrot tulips grab a lot of attention, and this one boasts heavily frilled and scalloped petals in a striking color combo. Rose, lemon-yellow and mandarin-red petals flecked with green grow on 17- to 21-inch stems.

WHY WE LOVE IT: The petals are extremely full and showy with their exotically frilly edges.

BLOOM TIME: Mid- to late spring.

5 Best Cottage-style: *Yellow Present*

Zones 3 to 8

At first blush, this tulip may not seem all that special, but it's truly a gift to your garden. Very strong and stout, it stands up to tough weather on its 12- to 14-inch stems. And if you look more closely, you'll see that its creamy yellow exterior and sunny golden interior make quite the pretty package.

WHY WE LOVE IT: It is one of the toughest Triumph tulips available and is more perennial than many others.

BLOOM TIME: Mid- to late spring.

6 Best New Variety: *Mystic van Eijk*

Zones 3 to 8

This new Darwin hybrid is a wonderful combination of old-fashioned pink and dark pinkish-red flames, making it a fascinating addition to your late-spring garden. The long-lasting blooms on 16- to 18-inch stems look lovely in bouquets.

WHY WE LOVE IT: These strong, sturdy stems are healthy and one of the best perennial tulips, flowering for several seasons.

BLOOM TIME: Mid- to late spring.

7 Best Mini: *Lady Jane*

Zones 3 to 8

The candy-striped petals are a delicious rose-red with bright white interiors. Growing only 8 to 10 inches tall, it's ideal for spring beds and borders—and you'll like its tendency to return year after year.

WHY WE LOVE IT: On sunny spring days, the flower opens fully to expose its brilliant white interior.
BLOOM TIME: Mid- to late spring.

8 Best Traditional: *Pink Impression*

Zones 3 to 8

The most popular tulips tend to be the standards, such as this beautiful bright pink one. Simple yet stunning, it blends several shades of rose and stands large and impressive on strong 20- to 22-inch stems.
WHY WE LOVE IT: As a Darwin hybrid, this tulip is more perennial than others. It is large, showy and really stands out in the garden.
BLOOM TIME: Mid-spring.

9 Best Double Bloom: *Monsella*

Zones 3 to 8

With its sweet scent and riot of color, this double early tulip turns heads in the garden. Canary-yellow petals are streaked with blood-red flames. It's a tough little flower, growing on strong 12-inch stems, and quite long-lasting in the garden.
WHY WE LOVE IT: It's among the earliest double tulips and also forces without much fuss.
BLOOM TIME: Early spring.

10 Best Tall: *Perestroyka*

Zones 3 to 8

This giant egg-shaped tulip is a stunning late bloomer. When it first opens, you see scarlet, muted orange and yellow, but from a distance the flower is a lovely, dusky salmon-rose color. At 24 to 30 inches, it towers over most other blooms.
WHY WE LOVE IT: It grows tall and strong, making it an excellent cut flower mixed with other late-spring blooms in a bouquet.
BLOOM TIME: Late spring.

don't dig it

After all your hard work planting bulbs, the critters got to them? Here are some ideas to combat common culprits:

DEER: Try a folded piece of chicken wire around the edge of your garden. They also might be deterred by anything with a human or cosmetic smell (hair, soap, etc.). Pepper spray can help but needs to be reapplied after it rains.

VOLES: Try spraying Ropel, Deer Off, Plantskydd or other bad-tasting substances on bulbs and allow to dry before planting. Then surround the bulbs with sharp crushed gravel.

SQUIRRELS AND CHIPMUNKS: Try placing chicken wire over the newly planted bulbs and securing with mulch or leaves.

perennials
for fall color

Bring a glorious autumn blaze to your garden with these foliage favorites.

BY LORIE L. WEST

1

Each fall, I count on the same old things: asters and mums, mums and asters. Yet all around me, trees and shrubs burst into magnificent displays of fawn and gold, russet and rust, and reds from ruby to richest burgundy. It recently occurred to me: Why not bring nature's fireworks into my own garden?

It's so easy to do. To inspire you, too, we've listed our favorite perennials for fall color. Some make dramatic changes when temperatures drop, while others are more subtle. But each one will brighten your backyard and add autumn oomph to your garden.

1 Cranesbill geranium

Geranium wlassovianum, Zones 3 to 9
Don't confuse the Cranesbill geranium with the popular bedding plant grown as an annual across the country. Cranesbill, a perennial beauty, puts on a flower display early in the season, and its geranium foliage makes stunning color changes in fall and in areas with mild winters.
FALL COLOR: Set your garden on fire! If you love bold, blazing reds, *G. wlassovianum* will give you a thrilling autumn show.

2 Blackberry Ice coral bells

Heuchera dolce 'Blackberry Ice', Zones 4 to 9
When it comes to gorgeous foliage, you can't go wrong with coral bells. Blackberry Ice, introduced just this year, simply redefines purple. New leaves emerge a vivid iridescent violet with branching black veins, while a paler amethyst graces the undersides.
FALL COLOR: As the leaves mature, they mellow into a pewter-purple color that lingers long into fall.

3 Miniature fountain grass

Pennisetum alopecuroides 'Burgundy Bunny', Zones 5 to 9
Does your small garden give you the fountain grass blues? Let this container-friendly miniature come to your rescue. Petite plumes wave gracefully above spiky green leaves. Burgundy Bunny is a favorite for the highlights of red in its summer foliage.
FALL COLOR: Fall sets this mini marvel ablaze in a fiery allover red that lasts until frost.

4 Autumn Brilliance fern

Dryopteris erythrosora 'Brilliance', Zones 5 to 9
In spring, this fern unfurls bright copper-colored fronds into a high-impact 2-foot-tall and -wide plant. The leaves grow green as summer sets in, which shifts attention to their interesting texture. Look no further for an intricate backdrop to bright blooms.
FALL COLOR: Watch this fern turn striking shades of orange and russet when the autumn temperature starts to drop.

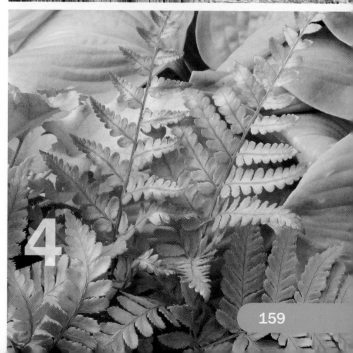

5 Autumn Frost hosta

Hosta 'Autumn Frost', Zones 3 to 9

You can't go wrong with a hosta when you're shopping for perennials with interesting fall color. This compact cultivar begins the growing season with leaves edged in bright yellow. They lighten in color as summer wears on, from strong gold to a soft, buttery hue. All shades complement the leaves' blue-green centers beautifully.

FALL COLOR: True to its name, this hosta's leaves turn to frosty white along the margins as fall approaches.

6 Arkansas amsonia

Amsonia hubrichtii, Zones 4 to 9

Feathery and fun, this amsonia grows into a medium-size bush of bottlebrush stems bearing silky needles. The effect is a softly blurred texture in the landscape, the perfect touch wherever you want to add a gentle, comforting effect.

FALL COLOR: Shades of gold and yellow engulf the entire plant as summer turns to autumn.

7 Angelina sedum

Sedum rupestre 'Angelina', Zones 3 to 11

Sedums always seem to come in handy, whether you have a large, sunny area to cover, a rock wall that demands plants good at finding a foothold, or a container that begs for an evergreen spiller. This ground cover forms an attractive yellow-green mat of texture in summer.

FALL COLOR: Watch the tips of the needlelike leaves blush a ginger brown and then red in colder temperatures, and you'll know this sedum is perfect for a dash of fall color.

8 Golden Japanese forest grass

Hakonechloa macra 'All Gold', Zones 5 to 8

A pleasingly shaggy mound of neon-chartreuse leaves, this All Gold variety is our choice of Japanese forest grass when it comes to color. Plant it in light to dappled shade and really set off your darker hostas and coral bells. Best of all, when a breeze comes through, the leaves will ripple gracefully and make gentle music.

FALL COLOR: When you see how these leaves turn a gorgeous straw-gold, it'll be hard to wait for next fall.

9 Early bergenia

Bergenia crassifolia, Zones 4 to 8

It's pretty, it's hardy and it's fun: Rub a leaf between your fingers and you'll learn why it's often called pig squeak! Early bergenia's round, leathery leaves make a lovely low ground cover. True to its name, it sends pretty magenta-pink blooms shooting up like little umbrellas starting in early spring.

FALL COLOR: The spoon-shaped leaves take on a bronze glow as winter begins. In mild zones, the plant may reflower.

10 Great Solomon's seal

Polygonatum canaliculatum, Zones 3 to 9

Yes, sometimes bigger is better! This aptly named plant grows to great heights, with arching stems that can reach up to 5 feet. Alternating leaves, which can grow roughly the size of an adult hand, add grace and texture that set off the yellow-white summer blooms.

FALL COLOR: From tip to tip, the entire plant softens into a striking gold, sporting beautiful berries of dark bluish-purple.

Croton

Planning for Fall Color

The time to think—and dream—about autumn color is in the fall. Walk around your property as the gardening year winds down and take a long, hard look. Think about where you'd like lively color.

Then stroll around your neighborhood, looking for fall landscapes you admire. Your neighbors are often your best resource, and you'll know that the plant you like thrives in your area.

Other resources for discovering the best plants for fall color are the nursery, public gardens and parks, the Internet and reference books. If a plant has fall foliage worth praising, someone's out there talking about it.

9

10

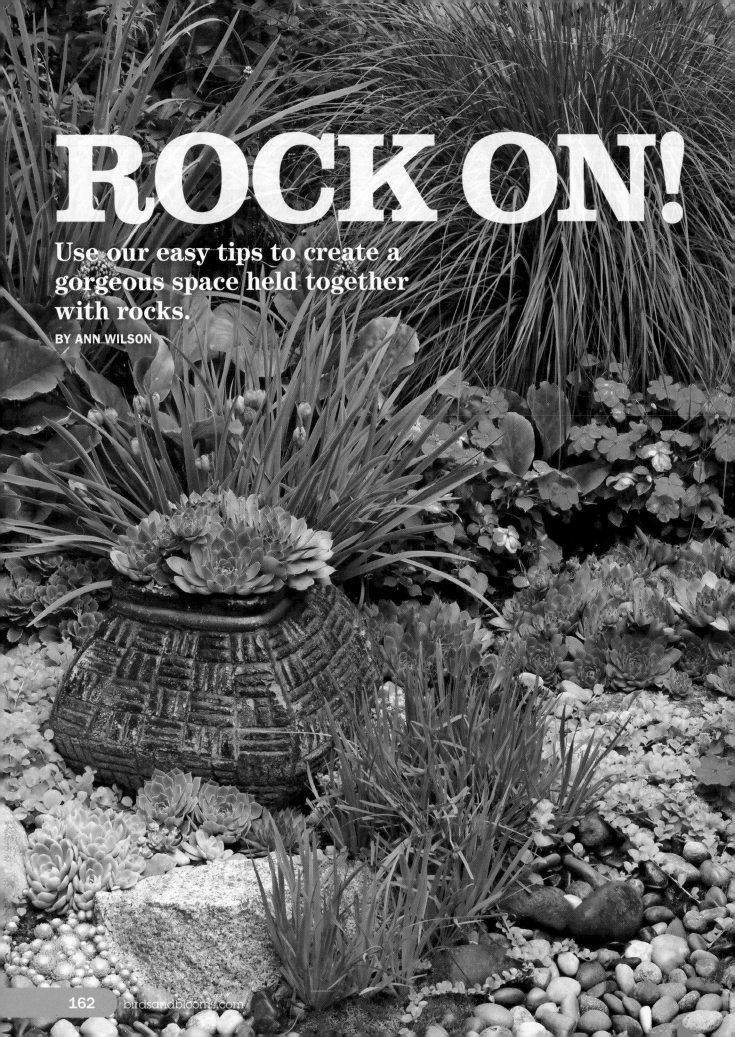

ROCK ON!

Use our easy tips to create a gorgeous space held together with rocks.

BY ANN WILSON

Houseleek

Start Small
You don't need a lot of space to start a rock garden. Find a corner of your yard or garden and give it a try to see if it suits you first.

Rock gardens expand a gardener's planting palette and offer creative challenges to gardening enthusiasts. Ideally suited to hot spots and difficult-to-tame slopes, they take their inspiration from wild flora that sprouts along gravelly mountain peaks and sandy desert floors.

Home Advantage

Rock gardening allows gardeners to play with an array of small plant varieties that would likely be lost if planted in traditional perennial borders.

Ed Glover, a member of the Wisconsin-Illinois chapter of the North American Rock Garden Society, has been rock gardening for more than 25 years. He tends his own 120- by 15-foot rock garden at his home and acts as a volunteer rock-garden caretaker at the University of Wisconsin-Madison.

"I like rock gardening because it's challenging," Ed says. "It allows me to try to grow plants I've seen in the mountains out west. Since the plants are small, you can put in lots of different ones in smaller areas. They supply pretty foliage when not in bloom, and the rocks are interesting, even in winter. I always tell people to start with a small rock garden. If they like it, they can expand it a little at a time."

Kim Zoss, a horticulturist at the Chicago Botanic Garden, also encourages gardeners to start small.

"Beginners might try cultivating a rock garden in a trough, in a nook, atop a small berm or around a water feature," Kim says. "Rock gardens should look like a natural part of the landscape, so a gardener needs to look at the whole yard to see how a rock garden will fit in. It's best to place the gardens where you can see them easily and often."

Location and Construction

As a rule, rock gardens require sunny sites and quick-draining soil. Ed recommends planting alpine-type gardens on sunny, south-facing slopes; xeric-type rock gardens planted with drought-tolerant plants do well where conditions are hot and dry.

"When constructing a rock garden, always build up for good drainage," Ed advises. "Instead of digging up existing soil, mound new soil atop the ground. I use a soil mix that's equal parts compost, sharp sand and pea gravel. Dig into the mix to place your rocks, and bury the bottom third of each rock, so it doesn't look like you just tossed the rocks in."

Burying portions of the rocks not only provides a natural overall appearance but also encourages plants to stretch their roots to the soil beneath the rocks, which results in healthier plants. Ed suggests spacing rocks to create crevices for tucking in cushion-forming plants or creeping cultivars that will wander over nearby stones. Situate larger rocks so they create microclimates that offer shaded planting sites on one side and sunny spots on the other. Tilt flat rocks to direct rainwater into the soil.

Select a single type of native rock in different sizes and shapes for a cohesive, natural-looking garden.

If you're planting alpine gardens, opt for porous

rocks such as limestone, sandstone, shale or tufa; nonporous rocks like marble, basalt and granite work well in desert-inspired gardens.

The Fun Part—Plant Selection

Common landscape-design principles—such as including zone-hardy varieties with varying heights, forms, textures and bloom times—apply when creating rock gardens. But because rock gardening focuses on individual plants, it's important to not crowd plants and to choose nonaggressive plants that won't overgrow their designated spots. If you're including evergreens for winter interest, select miniature varieties with a very slow growth rate.

Ed plants an array of alpine and subalpine perennials, many with cushionlike profiles. Draba aizoides, a mat-forming perennial with yellow flowers, and saxifrage, a silvery-foliaged plant with white, yellow or pink blooms, kick off the flower show in early spring. Creeping phlox and rock cress will blossom next and are followed by summer-blooming dianthus and blue-flowering campanula.

Desert rock gardens supply a good foundation for penstemons, sedums, cacti, low-growing yarrow and hens-and-chicks. The Chicago Botanic Garden's rock garden combines alpine and xeric perennials, such as ice plant, small sedums, ground-cover potentilla, pulsatilla, moss phlox and dwarf iris, with miniature evergreens, such as Teddy arborvitae. Other good rock-garden options include Tom Thumb cotoneaster and blue rug juniper, Kim says.

Perennials are the mainstay of rock gardens, but some gardeners incorporate heat-loving annuals, such as moss rose or creeping zinnia, into their design for season-long color. Kim

Dwarf iris

Hens-and-chicks

Saxifrage

Pulsatilla

ROCK STARS

Dwarf iris, hens-and-chicks, pulsatilla and saxifrage are all good starter plants to try in your rock garden.

also recommends tucking miniature spring bulbs amid the rocks for early spring color.

Rock gardening is becoming increasingly popular, and local nurseries are responding to the growing demand for rock-garden plants. Ed and Kim recommend checking local nurseries first—you'll often find plants larger than those available through mail-order catalogs and varieties specifically suited to your planting zone.

Care and Maintenance

After the plants are in, mulch the entire garden with at least an inch of gravel that matches your rocks and stones. The mulch conserves moisture, keeps weeds down and fashions a suitably stony backdrop for both boulders and plants. Limit fertilizer applications to once a year to keep plants from growing too large.

Educate yourself about each plant's water requirements—too much moisture may cause root rot; too little water may stress out plants. Instead of using a sprinkler, Kim suggests spot-watering each plant to meet its individual water needs adequately.

Yarrow, campanula and creeping phlox are all good options if you want to add spots of color.

Rock gardens don't have to be drab. You can find lots of little nooks and crannies to add spots of color.

Yarrow

Campanula

Creeping phlox

FACING PAGE, ROCK GARDEN: GAP PHOTOS/MARION BRENNER; HENS-AND-CHICKS: PROVEN WINNERS; REMAINING PHOTOS: RDA-GID; THIS PAGE, ROCK GARDEN: MARK TURNER/TURNER PHOTOGRAPHICS; REMAINING PHOTOS: WALTERS GARDEN INC.

glad you asked!

Gardening expert Melinda Myers answers your questions.

An old superstition in Maine says that if you point your index finger at a daffodil, it won't bloom.

▲ **My daffodils haven't bloomed in two seasons. If I dig them up and replant them, is there a chance they might blossom?**
Debbie Coutre COLCHESTER, ILLINOIS

MELINDA: Late spring frosts, overcrowding and heavy shade can keep daffodils from flowering. Prevent early sprouting by planting them away from the house's foundation, applying winter mulch after the ground freezes and selecting mid-spring-blooming varieties. It's worth the effort to dig, divide and replant daffodils. Make sure the leaves stay intact for at least six to eight weeks after flowering so the plant can produce and store energy for next year's blooms.

◄ **I've called this plant a blood lily. It blooms once a year, usually in May. What is this bulb really called?**
Dorothy Fuhrmeister
CLAYTON, GEORGIA

MELINDA: Your beautiful blood lily is a member of the amaryllis family and goes by the botanical name *Scadoxus multiflorus*. It is reliably hardy in Zones 8 to 10, and in some Zone 7 gardens with good drainage and the help of winter mulch. Grow this bulb in full sun or partial shade in well-drained soil. Those gardening in colder climates should grow bulbs in containers, since these plants don't like their roots disturbed. Gradually reduce watering in late summer, and move the containers indoors before the first fall frost. Then overwinter the dormant bulb in a cool, dry place.

How do you take seeds from plants like morning glory or foxglove?
Michele Palocy SYRACUSE, NEW YORK

MELINDA: In both cases, wait for the flowers to fade and capsules to develop. Harvest the morning glory seeds when the capsule is dry. Break it open, remove the seeds and allow them to dry for several weeks. Harvest the dried seed capsules on foxgloves when the bottom capsules start to break open. If you wait too long, the capsules shatter and seeds are dispersed in the garden. Dry the seeds thoroughly before storing.

Place seeds in envelopes, label with the plant name and date, then store in an airtight jar in the refrigerator. Start seeds indoors for earlier blooming in the garden. Morning glory seeds need to be soaked overnight in warm water or scarified by nicking the hard seed coat to encourage germination. Start the seeds as you would other flower and vegetable seeds.

Why do my purple coneflowers have only the reddish-brown centers this year? There are no purple petals.
Bill Diehl CINCINNATI, OHIO

MELINDA: Aster yellows is the culprit. This disease is caused by a phytoplasma, a bacteriumlike organism that attacks more than 300 species of plants, including coreopsis, marigolds, coneflowers, carrots and potatoes, causing discolored and distorted growth.

The disease-causing organism is spread by the aster leafhopper. As this insect feeds, it transfers the disease from infected to healthy plants. Remove infected plants to prevent the disease from spreading to your healthy ones. This disease rarely kills the plant, but the phytoplasma survives in it, which can cause future infection. Fortunately, coneflowers readily reseed, and regular sanitation can help you manage this disease.

▶ Do you have any suggestions for a rosebush? I'm looking for double blooms, light pink and fragrant. I do have a great deal of shade and can offer only half-day sun.
Kathy Bowles NORTHWOOD, OHIO

MELINDA: A good place to start is David Austin roses, from an English breeder whose products are widely available. He has several shade-tolerant, repeat-blooming varieties with fragrant pink flowers. Harlow Carr has an old-rose fragrance and grows to 4 feet tall, while Queen of Sweden is a bit smaller, with flowers that smell like myrrh.

Another option is rugosa rose. Several varieties of these disease-resistant roses fit your requirements. Jens Munk has a light fragrance and grows 4½ feet tall and wide. Theresa Bugnet grows double, fragrant pink flowers. Or try Morden Centennial, of the Canadian Parkland series of roses, for a fragrant, hardy option that will tolerate light shade.

The Queen of Sweden rose is available from David Austin roses.

How can I store begonias over the winter?
Dick Orlawski LUCK, WISCONSIN

MELINDA: Tuberous begonias can be grown as houseplants in a warm, sunny window if it's free from drafts of hot and cold air. You can also store the tuber in a cool, dark location for winter. Start by digging the tuber after a light frost. Allow it to dry for several days and then gently remove any excess soil and the dried foliage. Pack the tubers in peat moss and store in a cool 50-degree location for the winter.

FAQ
"I have sandy soil. What kinds of plants will grow well in it?"
Wanda Salsman LAKEWOOD, COLORADO

MELINDA: Look for drought-tolerant plants. You may need to water them several times a week to get them established, but once they're well-rooted, they'll tolerate the dry growing conditions. For sunny areas, try some of the following annuals: sunflower, zinnia, blanket flower, cosmos, cockscomb, gazania (treasure flower), portulaca, dusty miller, Dahlberg daisy, verbena and Mexican sunflower.

If you prefer perennials, try these sun lovers: purple coneflower, black-eyed Susan, gayfeather, thyme, artemisia, perennial sunflower, yucca, sedum, Russian sage, potentilla and ornamental grasses.

It's harder to find shade plants that will tolerate dry soil. Try perennials like deadnettle (*Lamium*), variegated archangel (*Lamium galeobdolon*), and coral bells. Annuals such as annual vinca and the biennial Chinese forget-me-nots will also grow in dry, partially shaded locations.

William Rollison potentilla

Morning glory
Photo by Marg Cousens/GAP Photos

Strawberry
Finalist in our Backyard Photo Contest
Photo by Katie Brenkert

Black-eyed Susan
Finalist in our Backyard Photo Contest
Photo by Christie Eden

Cleome
Finalist in our Backyard Photo Contest
Photo by Joan Bullock

Liatris
Finalist in our Backyard Photo Contest
Photo by Mae Dricken

WILLIAM LEAMAN/ALAMY

great
Escapes

Venture out to encounter the elusive birds you've always wanted to see. Read about the places that provide the best opportunities to spot your favorites. Get travel tips from fellow bird enthusiasts who have visited prime destinations.

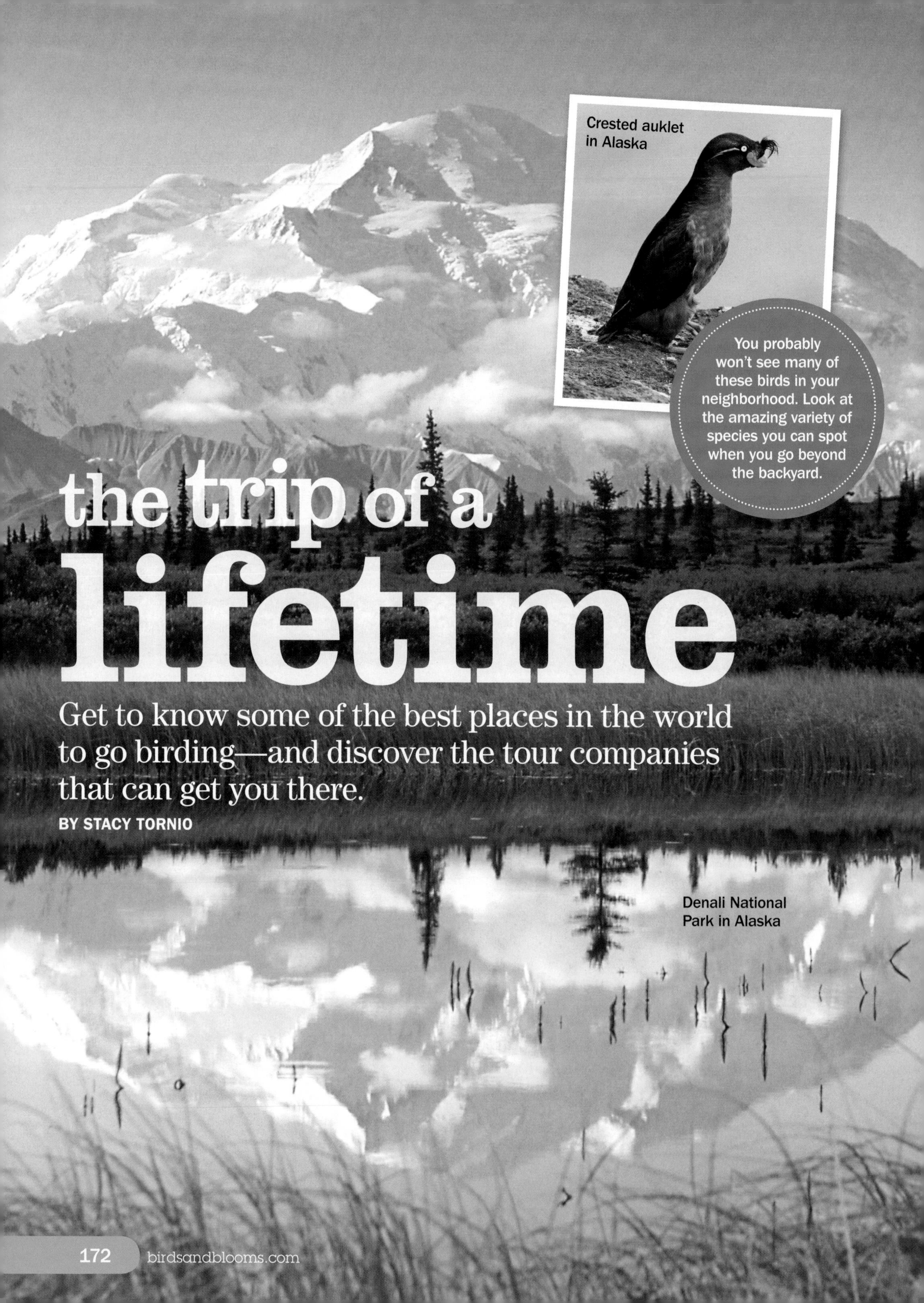

Crested auklet
in Alaska

You probably won't see many of these birds in your neighborhood. Look at the amazing variety of species you can spot when you go beyond the backyard.

the trip of a
lifetime

Get to know some of the best places in the world to go birding—and discover the tour companies that can get you there.

BY STACY TORNIO

Denali National
Park in Alaska

I need to start with a disclaimer. It's nearly impossible to pick only six places in the whole world to go birding. And it might be even harder to recommend just one tour company for each place.

Birding tourism is really booming. Dozens of companies seem to be popping up, promising you the best vacation ever, full of jaw-dropping birds from beginning to end.

While I've been to only one of these places myself (I adore Alaska), I really pulled out all the stops for this story, talking to bird experts and friends from around the country. After much research, I present you with these six great places to go, along with six great companies that can get you there.

If you're planning a birding adventure, I strongly encourage you to contact some of these companies and see how they might be able to help. Selecting a company to go birding with is a lot like buying new shoes. You can't go by looks alone; you really have to try them on. I mean, you're probably looking at spending thousands of dollars for one of these trips.

So contact these companies and try them on for size—ask them questions, get their advice, talk to them about what areas you want to visit. Chances are, you'll figure out just the right fit for you and will soon be on your way to the trip of a lifetime.

Alaska

It's easy to see why people call Alaska the last frontier. It truly is a majestic piece of wilderness that has remained largely untouched. Anyone who has been there knows how special it is— and it's a pretty special place for birds as well.

Many birding trips to Alaska go to Gambell, on the northwest tip of St. Lawrence Island in the Bering Sea. (Once you're this far west, you can actually see Russia if you have clear weather.) You'll see a wide range of seabirds here, such as the tufted puffin, as well as many other species, like the spectacled eider, white wagtail, red-necked stint, dusky warbler and hoary redpoll.

Beyond Gambell, you'll find a whole slew of other arctic birds waiting for you. Yes, Alaska is big (roughly 20 percent the size of the Lower 48), but try to soak up as much as you can while you're there. From the birds to the other wildlife to the astounding scenery, it will be one of your best trips ever.

CHECK OUT: A company called WINGS pioneered bird travel to Alaska, and many others have followed in its footsteps. WINGS has been around since the 1970s and has a wide range of tours all over the world, including

Snowy owl in Canada

Tufted puffin in Alaska

Birders near Nome, Alaska

King eider in Canada

A great jacamar (above) and a fiery-billed aracari (right) are both birds you'd see in Panama.

several options with its sister company in the United Kingdom, Sunbird Tours. Its groups are small and the guides are some of the best in the business. Learn more at *wingsbirds.com*.

Canada

There's some superb birding just over the border. Like Alaska, Canada is rich in untouched wilderness areas, each with its own wildlife. Love owls? You can find a tour devoted just to these special birds. How about a trip specializing in whales and birds, or polar bears and birds? Yep, you can find those, too.

One of the highlights is the Canadian tundra above the Arctic Circle, where you'll find far northern birds like the yellow-billed loon, the king eider and a wide range of northern owls.

CHECK OUT: Eagle-Eye Tours is a bit smaller than other companies but has exceptional offerings and leaders. Based in Canada, it offers trips all across the country, as well as to Greenland, New Zealand and more. Take a look at its site (*eagle-eye.com*) to get a feel for the company and its personalized approach to bird travel.

Belize

Tourism in Belize is at an all-time high, and the locals are welcoming birders with open arms. This tiny country (it's only 170 miles long) has fewer than 300,000 people and has managed to preserve enormous sections of habitat for all kinds of wildlife. With nearly 600 species of birds alone, you'll discover loads you never knew of.

The Belize Audubon Society, *belizeaudubon.org*, is the place to start if you want to learn about the country and the birds you'll find there. It'll point you toward wildlife sanctuaries that are home to species like the ornate hawk-eagle, the boat-billed heron and the American pygmy kingfisher. And don't forget to look for tropical birds like the scarlet macaw and the keel-billed toucan, which is the national bird of Belize.

CHECK OUT: Belize is a hot spot, so you'll find lots of tour companies. Our favorite is Wildside Nature Tours (*wildsidenaturetours.com*). Owner Kevin Loughlin started Wildside after a trip to Belize more than 20 years ago. The country changed his life, and now he wants to share that passion with others.

Panama

Panama is a big tourist destination and, increasingly, a retirement choice for American baby boomers. Still, it values its biodiversity so highly that it has set aside more than a quarter of its land for national parks and refuges.

That and the tropical climate mean that an amazing 900 species of birds spend all or part of the year here. You'll see all kinds of toucans, puffbirds, hummingbirds, jacamars, woodcreepers, antbirds and more. In fact, it's easy to spot more than 100 bird species in a single day.

NEED HELP?
The Nature Travel Network is a wonderful new online resource. Visit *naturetravelnetwork.com* for all kinds of helpful travel information.

Blue-footed booby in the Galapagos

CHECK OUT: Pretty much all bird tour companies go to Panama, but we like the small mom-and-pop operation Cheepers! Birding on a Budget. Owners Cindy and Jim Beckman do all the planning and paperwork, and they go on the tours, too. If you check out their website (*cheepersbirding.com*) and email an inquiry, you'll hear back directly from one of them.

South Africa

South Africa is simply one of the best places in the world to watch wildlife. It's also known for its wonderful diversity of wildflowers, good food, fine wines and friendly people.

You won't want to miss the "big five" of the savannas—lion, leopard, black rhinoceros, Cape buffalo and elephant—but be sure to leave enough time for the country's 800-plus birds, both coastal and inland. On a three-week trip, you could easily see 400 to 500 species. Among the many notable ones: rockjumpers, sugarbirds, African penguins, bald ibis, black harriers and orange-breasted sunbirds.

CHECK OUT: If you're thinking about South Africa, consider the bird tour company based there—Rockjumper Birding Tours. The staff knows the country inside and out, and quite a few other areas as well. Rockjumper does tours all over the world but loves showing people its own backyard. Learn more at *rockjumperbirding.com*.

Galapagos Islands

If you love the water, perhaps a bird cruise is more your style. The Galapagos, formed from volcanic ash and made famous by the explorations of Charles Darwin, are on the bucket list of even some nonbirders. With only about 25,000 people living here, you'll feel as if you have a little piece of heaven all to yourself.

The diversity of landscape is truly mind-boggling. Because of the way the islands have developed, land that just barely reaches sea level is juxtaposed with mountains more than 5,000 feet tall. Isabela Island is the largest in the collection at around 62 miles long. Some of the birds you're sure to see are penguins, cormorants and the outrageously photogenic blue-footed booby.

Chances are you'll fly to Ecuador before your trip to the Galapagos. The country boasts some of the best birding in South America, giving you the perfect excuse to add some more species to your life list before or after you tour the Galapagos.

CHECK OUT: Victor Emanuel Nature Tours (VENT) is one of the largest and best-known international bird tour companies. Victor Emanuel started the company more than 30 years ago and has earned the respect and admiration of some of the best birders in the world. The company offers so many kinds of tours that you can easily spend hours on its website (*ventbird.com*) planning your next adventure.

Blue-throated toucanet in Panama

Diederik cuckoo in Africa

Red-lored parrot in Belize

birders' bucket list

When it comes to birding in North America, these must-see places top the list.

BY STACY TORNIO

A really good vacation provides a temporary escape from the stresses of everyday life. A really great vacation? Well, it involves birding.

As the editor of *Birds & Blooms*, I get to see a lot of beautiful pictures of birds. But it's a whole other thing to see them in person. That's why, when I travel, I'm always looking for new species. On a recent trip to Arizona, I spotted a pyrrhuloxia for the first time, and I can tell you, finding a new bird is an adventure...and good for the soul, too.

I asked my most knowledgeable birding friends around the country what destinations they thought should be on every birder's "bucket list." While there certainly are outstanding birding locales in all 50 states and across Canada, these top 10 are in a class by themselves. Which one(s) might become a stop for your next trip?

Unique marvels in the Rio Grande Valley

Texas' Rio Grande Valley is one of the best places to find those elusive species, such as the gorgeous green jay, that can be seen only in the southernmost tips of the U.S. This area is also the home of the World Birding Center, *theworldbirdingcenter.com*. To get the most bang for your travel buck, we suggest visiting in November, during the area's annual birding festival. Learn more at *rgvbf.org*.

TEXAS

Golden-fronted woodpeckers in Rio Grande Valley

Great egrets in the Everglades

Hummingbirds in southeast Arizona

ARIZONA

Touted as the Hummingbird Capital of the World, the area around Sierra Vista and Ramsey Canyon is where you'll want to focus your quest for rare hummingbirds. Home to an amazing 15 hummer species, it boasts spring and summer regulars like the calliope, rufous and broad-tailed. But during spring and fall migration, which is when we recommend going, you can also see rarities like the white-eared, blue-throated and berylline. Many tour companies and local businesses cater to hummingbird lovers, but we suggest starting your trip planning at *visitsierravista.com*.

Florida's best in the Everglades

FLORIDA

Covering nearly 1.5 million acres, this fabled swamp is the largest subtropical wilderness in the nation, making it an ideal habitat for manatees, crocodiles, Florida panthers and, of course, things with wings. Many species winter here, so it's not hard to find less common visitors like the frigatebird in addition to the regulars such as anhingas, flycatchers and warblers. Just put "birding in the Everglades" in your search engine, and you'll be delightfully overwhelmed.

White-eared hummingbird, Arizona

Bird-watchers in Cape May

Shorebirds in Cape May

Cape May Bird Observatory is one of the best-known facilities of its kind in North America. You can find activities year-round at Cape May, including the World Series of Birding in May and an autumn birding festival. Located on the southern tip of New Jersey, the cape is a paradise for lovers of shorebirds. There's hardly a wrong time to visit this hot spot, so start the planning at *birdcapemay.com*.

NEW JERSEY

Warblers in northwest Ohio

OHIO

Ohio? Really? I thought the same thing, but just one trip turned me into a believer. While May is the perfect month to look for warblers throughout much of North America, visiting the area around Toledo gives you a chance to see many different warblers in one place. The area hosts the annual Biggest Week in American Birding festival, where some visitors in 2012 saw a Kirtland's warbler, among the rarest of the rare. Book rooms early, as hotels sell out. Start planning at *biggestweek inamericanbirding.com*.

Kirtland's warbler

Birders on Attu Island

Sandhill cranes in Nebraska

You've never seen sandhill cranes until you've seen them like this. Thousands of cranes—80 percent of the world's sandhill population, in fact—descend upon the Platte River in mid- to late March. You'll see plenty of ducks and geese, too. While many places claim to offer excellent crane sightings, Nebraska really does take top honors. Begin your adventure at *nebraskaflyway.com*.

Rare birds on Alaska's Attu Island

OK, let's be honest. The weather is horrible, with only a handful of clear days each year. The trip will cost you more than $7,000. The accommodations aren't exactly luxurious. But the location? Ah, the location. Though technically part of Alaska, Attu is in the Eastern Hemisphere, closer to Russia than to the United States. You may have seen this once-in-a-lifetime trip featured in the 2011 birding movie *The Big Year*. If you go, as the characters in the movie did, you'll see rare and amazing species that other birders in North America can only dream of. Did somebody say whiskered auklet? You'll need to sign up for a tour to get to Attu; get more information at *zbirdtours.com*.

Diversity in Utah

You'll find a spectacular array of habitats here, from subalpine mountain, forest and sage-steppe to upland, wetland and desert. And, as you'll learn at *visitutah.com*, you can get to them all in the same day! Bear River Migratory Bird Refuge in northern Utah, where the Bear River flows into the Great Salt Lake, is a good place to start. Several marshes here are protected, making them prime spots for waterfowl and other western birds. Get more information and see a bird report powered by *ebird.org* at *fws.gov/bearriver*.

American avocet foraging at Bear River in Utah

Atlantic puffin on
the coast of Maine

Puffins on the Maine coast

If you look at a range map, you'll see that
Atlantic puffins live mostly at sea, making
it a little difficult for us land dwellers to spot
these unique, bright-beaked birds. But there
is a way. In spring and summer, they come
ashore to nest and raise their young—though
you'll still need to hop on a boat to view them.
The thriving puffin population most people
go to see is located near Muscongus Bay,
Maine. Learn more about these birds and the
tour companies that offer trips to see them at
projectpuffin.org. And who knows? You just
might see some roseate terns, seals or even
whales along the way, too!

MAINE

Unique birds in Hawaii

Hawaii is on many bucket
lists for all kinds of reasons,
but the birding here is truly
special. Each island boasts
its own wealth of species.
A good place to start figuring
out what you want to see
is *hawaiiaudubon.org*.
You can also find lots of
independent companies
offering birding tours, so
do your homework online
before you go—and get
ready to start checking off
tropical beauties like the
'I'iwi from your life list.

The 'I'iwi with 'Ohi'a
flowers in Hawaii

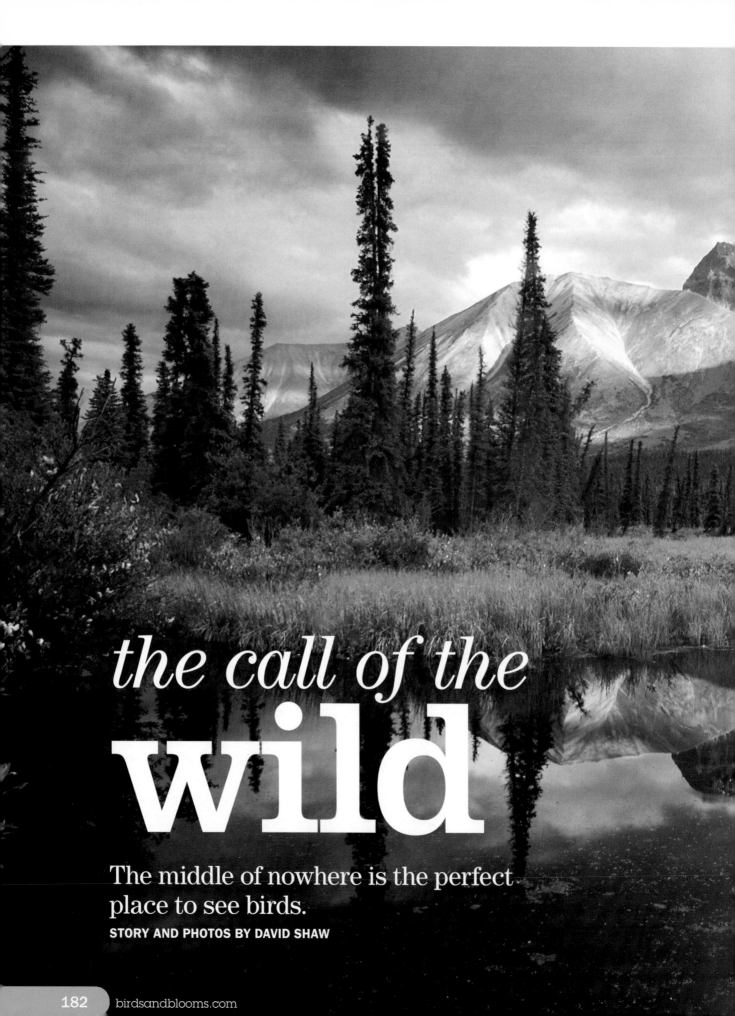

the call of the
wild

The middle of nowhere is the perfect place to see birds.

STORY AND PHOTOS BY DAVID SHAW

This serene scene shows the wilderness of Nabesna Road in Alaska.

Boreal chickadees call the boreal forest of Canada home and are rarely spotted in the U.S.

Rain came down in torrents, making the tropical rain forest nearly invisible. Huge logs bobbed in the swollen, churning river.

Sitting in the bow of a 20-foot dugout canoe, I was drenched, clutching my plastic-wrapped camera bag and listening to the outboard motor cough and backfire. I figured our chances of capsizing and ending up in the seething river were excellent.

Through both my work as a wilderness guide and my sheer love of nature, I find myself in this sort of scenario a lot. Yet, despite the terrifying canoe rides (they've all ended safely so far), the days spent shivering in a rain-lashed tent on the tundra and the pain of blisters that rise on my feet after too many rocky miles of trail, I return to these wild places again and again.

Slowing the Clock

A journey into the wilderness is a bit like time travel. You go from the noisy, busy domain of people and their machines to a world that moves at a different pace. There is change in the wild— seasons shift, birds migrate, trees grow and die— but it all happens gradually. Immersing yourself in this slow-motion world is one of the joys of travel to remote places.

Each summer I guide wilderness backpacking and river trips into Alaska's Brooks Range. It is staggeringly beautiful country, with sweeping valleys, rugged peaks and rivers clear as glass. There are few trees, and the views seem endless. Birds migrate unimpeded up and down the valleys and over the mountains to the vast expanse of wet tundra on Alaska's North Slope.

Into the Wild

When you go birding in the Brooks Range, or anywhere in the wilderness, there are no scope-bearing hordes, no cellphones ringing to obscure the birds' songs, nothing to interrupt as you watch a falcon play the wind. The birds you find are yours alone.

This is a different kind of birding experience from what many are used to. You're not chasing a rarity or luring it to your feeder. You're watching birds in their own world.

Perhaps because true wilderness is difficult to reach, you appreciate every bird you see or hear. During the summer around my home in Fairbanks, Alaska, I hear many species singing: yellow-rumped warblers, ruby-crowned kinglets, dark-eyed juncos, white-crowned sparrows, boreal and black-capped

The Wild Picks

David recommends these top five places to visit for wilderness birding.

1. THE ARCTIC NATIONAL WILDLIFE REFUGE. This vast, wild, beautiful Alaskan refuge should top anyone's list for both wilderness exploring and unsurpassed birding. Explore the coastal plain in June for nesting shorebirds and waterfowl, or the mountains of the Brooks Range for such rarities as northern wheatear and Smith's longspur.

2. THE ROCKY MOUNTAINS. The Rockies extend through a number of states, each with its own hot spots. White-tailed ptarmigan, Lewis's woodpeckers and black rosy-finches are among the many birding highlights.

3. BIG BEND NATIONAL PARK. The mountainous deserts of West Texas—and in particular the wild areas of Big Bend—make for an incredible birding destination. The Colima warbler and several other species are found in the U.S. only in the mountains of Big Bend, and the greater roadrunner, black-chinned sparrow and blue-throated hummingbird are not to be missed.

4. THE CHIRICAHUA NATIONAL MONUMENT. Southern Arizona is a mecca for birders. The most prized species are the elegant trogon and the magnificent hummingbird, but there are countless others to see. Miles of hiking trails are a big draw, too.

5. EVERGLADES NATIONAL PARK. Well-known as a birding paradise for its many species of waders, the Everglades is also a wonderful place to find a bit of wilderness. Miles of canoe routes provide access to backcountry camping near the park's bird-filled mangrove forests.

"Generally speaking, a howling wilderness does not howl: it is the imagination of the traveler that does the howling."

—*Henry David Thoreau*

A scrubby pine in Colorado's Front Range just outside of Denver

chickadees, varied thrushes and more. I hear these so often that the sounds can wash right over me, barely registering. But if I listen to those same songs in the wild, they sound entirely new. I'm tuned in, aware.

Capture the Moment

Photography, too, is different in wild places. Time and distance require you to be a minimalist. You can't carry every lens and gadget you do when shooting from your car or at home.

Some photographers I've talked to or guided find this limiting, but I think they're looking at it wrong. The challenge in photography has always been to compose only what is necessary. Cluttered images without focus or depth are rarely successful, and the ability to compose an image has little to do with equipment. These parameters can force you to consider the landscape and its inhabitants in a new way.

Sit down with the stones, tundra or river and wait. Observe the wildlife. Where do they linger? What do they avoid? Slowly, you can start making images. The first few usually aren't great, but eventually your photos will improve. And when you look back on the pictures, you'll remember the exquisite moments.

The Journey Home

When I get home—for a while, at least—the lessons of the wilderness stay with me. I hear the birds in my yard with renewed appreciation. I watch them flit in and out of my feeder and admire the sleek tuxedo of the black-capped chickadees. I catch the first subtle notes of a ruby-crowned kinglet's song.

But it goes beyond that. I remember that there are aspects of the wild everywhere. Migrating birds land in parks and backyards across the country. Flowers poke through cracks in the pavement; peregrine falcons nest atop skyscrapers. Wildness remains, and it's worth exploring.

A pair of tundra swans on the coastal plain of the Arctic National Wildlife Refuge

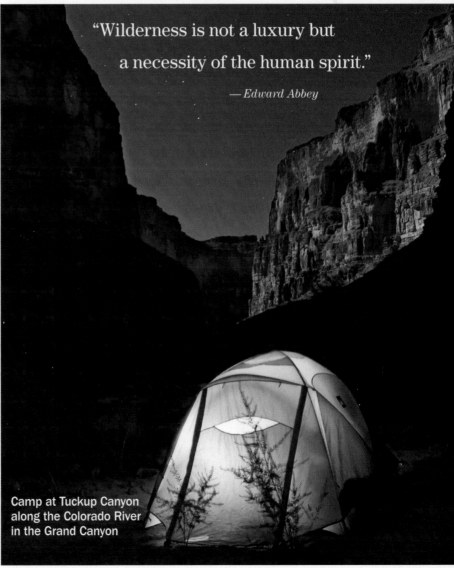

"Wilderness is not a luxury but a necessity of the human spirit."

— *Edward Abbey*

Camp at Tuckup Canyon along the Colorado River in the Grand Canyon

birding by canoe

...and train, bike and horse

Discover a whole new world of bird-watching on the go.

BY KIRSTEN SWEET

What if I told you that bird-watching could be even more exciting and adventurous than it already is? Don't get me wrong; I love strolling down a path through a local park or woods or along a body of water to see birds. But there are so many other ways to get up close and deep inside birds' environments—to places your feet alone can't take you.

Let me show you some of the intriguing possibilities and nontraditional experiences available to birders.

Paddle Downstream

For a simple change of pace, start with a birding canoe trip. They're easy to find, they're inexpensive (or sometimes even free), and you need very little experience with either canoeing or birding. Take it from me. On my first try, I nearly steered our digital editor into a low-hanging tree. (Sorry again, Danielle!) But we had a good time, saw a couple of eagles fly overhead and even had a few laughs as we paddled along.

You can find canoe trips for birders all over the country. The Atlanta Audubon Society, for instance, runs popular trips to see osprey and bald eagles in partnership with the Chattahoochee Nature Center. Look

around for an Audubon group or nature center in your area or on your next vacation and inquire.

Katie Andersen, an avid birder and kayaker from Erie, Pennsylvania, has been on dozens of these trips. In the water, where you can't stop on a dime, she likes to practice identifying birds by ear. And don't worry if you don't see what chirped, quacked or warbled. Experienced birders like Katie will tell you that if you heard it, it counts!

Look for an Audubon chapter near you at audubon.org.

Two-Wheeled Adventure

Strap on a helmet and hop on your bicycle! Oh, and don't forget the binoculars. You can bike in most of the same areas you'd walk, but you can cover more ground, opening up more possibilities. Be prepared to hop on and off your bike in a hurry, though, when you come across birds of interest.

A prime location for birding on two wheels is San Diego's Mission Bay. It's so popular, in fact, that the San Diego Bird Festival added a bicycle field trip to its lineup of events. And because that trip has been such a hit, the San Diego Audubon Society offers occasional free bike tours outside the festival dates.

Great blue herons can be seen year-round on the Verde Canyon train tours.

Try birding by kayak for a change of perspective.

Cruising for Birds

Sure, you can spot birds from a boat on any old lake, but there's something better: a private, customized tour through Everglades National Park on a shallow draft boat. Capt. Dave Hunt started visiting the park as a kid and just kept going back. Now, through his company, Everglades Birding, he takes one or two people out at a time, tailoring the itinerary to the birds his passengers want to see.

Brandon and Elissa Brywczynski of Delta, Ohio, recently returned from a trip with Capt. Dave and say that his knowledge and excitement were utterly infectious.

"Dave's trip netted me 12 new birds for the year, and seven of them were life birds," Brandon says. "He spotted a magnificent frigatebird with the naked eye that seemed to be miles away. Sure enough, when I got my glasses on it, that's what it was."

Book a trip with Capt. Dave Hunt by visiting *evergladesbirding.com*.

All Aboard!

Imagine this: You've just hopped aboard a restored vintage train and are seated in a comfy chair as eagles soar past the window. Verde Canyon Railroad in Clarkdale, Arizona, makes this a reality several times a week all year long. Birding by rail just

might be the most comfortable way to bird-watch—and you can even do it in first class, if you like!

Bald eagles, great blue herons and red-tailed hawks call the Verde Canyon home all year round. Complete with open-air observation cars and

attendants who are experts on the area, the train makes a four-hour round trip through the canyon. Birders may want to take advantage of the special Eagle Watch trips that promise excellent views during nesting season, January through April.

For more about the Verde Canyon Railroad, visit *verdecanyonrr.com*.

Giddyap!

Yes, it is what you think it is—birding on horseback. The number of organized tours out there is limited, but one with a particularly good reputation is Birds & Spurs at the Great Salt Lake Bird Festival in Farmington, Utah. Led by experienced wranglers, the ride is leisurely; you might see peregrine falcons, burrowing owls, grasshopper sparrows and several kinds of shorebirds.

According to festival head Neka Roundy, the horseback jaunt does a lot of repeat business. And because each tour is limited to six participants, it's an intimate experience. If it's on your list, make sure to sign up fast!

A juvenile flamingo in the Florida Everglades

Go It Alone

Don't care for group tours? No problem. Here are tips for bird-watching alone from Katie Andersen, who often goes birding in her kayak.

PUT SAFETY FIRST.
When birding by yourself, make sure others know where you are and when you plan to return. Wear a helmet or a life jacket if birding on a bike or a boat.

BE WATER-WISE.
A hat, sunglasses and sunscreen are a must if you're going to be on the water. Use brightly colored waterproof pouches for electronics, wallets, etc.

KNOW BEFORE YOU GO.
Before you head out, look at recent birding reports for the area so you know which species you might see and hear.

EQUIPMENT MATTERS.
Whether you're on horseback or paddling a canoe, you want your binoculars accessible but your hands free. A binocular harness is a smart investment for both ease and comfort.

incredible
Edibles

Go beyond your usual harvest and try delicious new fruits and veggies. Discover the health benefits of eating fresh-picked produce from the garden. Stock up on locally grown specialties at your area farmers market.

KONSTANTTIN/SHUTTERSTOCK.COM

you say *tomato,* I say *tomatillo*

Consider underappreciated vegetables every kitchen gardener should chew over.

BY HEATHER RAY

Tomatillos (here and left) and bok choy (right) are both tasty options for gardeners looking to try something new.

This might sound extreme, but I'm just gonna say it. There is life after tomatoes.

Stay with me now—most gardeners and chefs would agree that few things rival the anticipation of slicing into the sweet, taut flesh of your first homegrown tomato. But if you're itching to be a little adventurous, we have some great picks to turn your gardening neighbors green with envy— all while making you a hero in the kitchen.

This year, in addition to the recurrent tomatoes and cucumbers, check out a collection of unsung yet wildly delicious vegetables. Transforming the ordinary into extraordinary, these tasty alternatives are not your average backyard vegetables.

Instead of tomatoes...grow tomatillos

Say adios to the usual garden crop and get ready to be known for making the best salsa verde on the block. Growing tomatillos, a zesty staple in Mexican cuisine, is a simple way to stock your kitchen for a mighty tasty fiesta. These tangy members of the nightshade family grow inside a papery, husklike shell, resembling a Chinese lantern bloom. When they're ready for the party, the green shells turn brown and split open, yielding a green to yellow fruit.

Like tomatoes, tomatillo plants can quickly reach 3 feet tall, so stake them young. You'll need two or more plants for the blooms to be pollinated and fruit to be produced, and since the tiny yellow flowers attract bees, you'll have a few busy helpers to fertilize the flowers.

It's not grown for its looks, but celeriac is great for cooks.

Cucamelons are about the size of grapes.

Grow soybeans and you could make your own edamame.

CELERIAC: STOCKFOOD/SCHANZ; CUCAMELON: TERROIR SEEDS LLC./UNDERWOOD GARDENS; SOYBEANS: FOTOKOSTIC/SHUTTERSTOCK.COM; BEETS: PAUL MAGUIRE/SHUTTERSTOCK.COM; ARTICHOKES: SAXON HOLT

Instead of celery... grow celeriac

It has been called the ugly duckling of the vegetable world and is perhaps the most underappreciated vegetable in all the land. But what this hearty root lacks in appearance, it makes up for in versatility and taste. With a distinct celerylike flavor and interior ivory flesh, the easy-to-grow orb-shaped root can be peeled and chopped into cubes for use in soups and stews. Boiled and mashed, celeriac is a satisfying, nonstarchy alternative to mashed potatoes. The ugly duckling may not turn into a swan, but check out the Brilliant variety for its smooth skin and white flesh.

Instead of cabbage... grow bok choy

Asian stir-fries and salads just aren't the same without this delicate Chinese cabbage. The vegetable is grown from seed in spring and fall for its tender leaves and crunchy stalks. While Asian vegetables grow faster than Western types, bolting is a common problem—plants prematurely produce flowering stems before they're harvested (though the birds won't mind). This can hurt the edible portion of the plant, but luckily, bok choy can be grown as a cut-and-come-again crop. Varieties such as Joi Choi are more bolt-resistant than others.

Instead of cucumbers... grow cucamelons

The adorable gems dubbed cucamelons (*Melothria scabra*) resemble cute, dollhouse-sized watermelons. More properly known as Mexican sour gherkin, this newly rediscovered heirloom will reward your gardening efforts with crisp cucumber flavor accompanied by a zingy bite. Some people describe it as having a pickled flavor, making it a fun addition to sandwiches, salads and other dishes.

Cucamelons grow much like cucumbers but are more tolerant of cool weather. To discourage pests and provide support, install a cage or trellis roughly 6 inches from the plants.

Instead of green beans...grow soybeans

A nutritional powerhouse, this nutty-flavored legume yields nearly 15 grams of protein per half-cup, making it a favorite among vegetarian chefs. Plants grow about 2½ feet tall and have a rich color. They're ready to harvest when the beans inside the pods are thick and plump.

If you're really big on growing soybeans, the Midori Giant variety is considered to be the biggest soybean available to home gardeners, yielding two to three buttery 1¼-inch seeds per pod. A word of caution for eager tasters: Soybeans are potentially toxic when eaten raw, so be sure to boil or steam them before serving.

Instead of spinach... grow beets

Beets instead of spinach? Yes! Not only can you add a burst of color to your dinner plate with these nutrient-rich and deep-shaded roots, you can saute the leaves or toss them in salads as a delicious substitute for spinach. Roasted, boiled or pickled, these earthy-flavored roots are easy to grow and come in an assortment of colors. When sliced, varieties like Chioggia show off red and white rings that resemble a target.

Instead of potatoes... grow sweet potatoes

Potatoes are perhaps the world's most popular vegetable (330 million tons are produced globally every year) and are a common sight in backyard gardens. But if you're up for a new challenge, the rewards will be...well, sweet. A little tricky to grow, sweet potatoes need a long frost-free period and lots of sunshine.

When bought from mail-order suppliers, sweet potatoes arrive as slips—small unrooted cuttings from tubers that have sprouted. When they arrive, place them in a jar of water to perk them up, and be sure the last frost has passed before planting them outdoors. By the time late fall rolls around, you'll be able to kick back with your first batch of homegrown sweet potato fries.

Instead of onions... grow shallots

Meet every cook's best friend. While similar to onions in the way they grow, shallots differ in that a single set will produce more than 10 mildly sweet and subtle garlicky bulbs in just a few short months. Considering the surprisingly high price for shallots in supermarkets, the value for your money can't be beat—making them the best friend of budget-minded gardeners as well.

Wondering what variety to pick? Two that chefs often prefer for making vinaigrettes and bringing out the flavor of meat and seafood entrees are French Red and French Demi-Long.

With beets, you can eat both the roots and the lettucelike tops.

Here are some other less-frequently grown veggie varieties available to home gardeners. Out of 20, how many have you tried growing?

- Artichoke
- Arugula
- Asparagus
- Broccoli
- Brussels sprouts
- Chicory
- Eggplant
- Endive
- Garlic
- Honeydew
- Horseradish
- Kohlrabi
- Leeks
- Microgreens
- Mesclun
- Okra
- Peanuts
- Pumpkins
- Radish
- Turnip

So how did you fare?

0: This is sad

1-4: Be more adventurous

5-9: Not too shabby

10 or more: Garden guru

Artichokes are grown for beauty as much as for their veggie value.

top
10
fruit trees for small spaces

You don't need to own acres of orchards or live in the South to grow gorgeous fruit trees.

BY KIRSTEN SWEET

1

Sure, you can easily walk into the grocery store and toss a bag of nectarines or Honeycrisp apples into your shopping cart. But wouldn't it be better if you could just walk out your back door?

We found a new book, *Fruit Trees in Small Spaces* by Colby Eierman. It's all about fruit trees and how to grow them, care for them and—the most important part—how to reap the rewards. Best of all, these trees won't take over your yard. The dwarf options are endless, and some will even flourish in containers.

In our list below, we've suggested one variety for each type of fruit tree. But, as with any new plant you're going to try, make sure the one you choose will work in your zone and growing conditions. And keep in mind that some fruit trees, such as apples, require two plants for cross-pollination and fruit formation. Stop by your favorite nursery or local extension office to find out which varieties will do best in your backyard.

1 Grapefruit

In order for the grapefruit on a tree to get the brilliant color we all look for, it needs intense summer heat. But the color of the fruit doesn't determine its ripeness. If a grapefruit feels heavy on the tree, pluck it off and give it a try.

TRY THIS: The Rio Red bears sweet, seedless grapefruits that are ideal for juice. The dwarf form of this variety is perfect for a small space.

2 Apple

The many varieties of apple trees available can be a bit overwhelming, so it's especially important to find out what will work with your growing conditions. Be sure to look for disease-resistant trees, because apple trees are very susceptible to a number of ailments.

TRY THIS: You can't go wrong planting a Honeycrisp. Its sweet, crunchy, medium-size apples are perfect for eating right off the tree.

3 Mandarin

Only gardeners in the far South can enjoy the fruit of a mandarin tree straight from the backyard. But if you're in the right zone, they're fairly easy to grow. A mandarin will require some pruning to shape it into a tree or shrub, but other than that, just enjoy!

TRY THIS: Satsuma mandarin trees are a popular choice. They will produce large, sweet, easy-to-peel fruit.

4 Lime

Lime trees are very sensitive to cold, so make sure you can accommodate their needs before trying to grow one. Not only do these trees produce juicy fruit for cocktails and cooking, they have beautiful dark, glossy leaves.

TRY THIS: Mexican limes, also known as key limes, are more suitable for warm climates. They're upright trees that will grow up to 15 feet tall.

5 Apricot

Northern gardeners, this one's for you! Apricot trees do tolerate cold temperatures, but be careful. Because of early flowering, late frost can sometimes take its toll on trees. The fruit is delicate, so growing your own ensures you'll get high-quality, unblemished apricots.

TRY THIS: If you're looking for a sweet apricot, give Goldcot a try. It ripens midseason and is good for colder climates.

6 Pear

When it comes to pear trees, you've got a choice—European or Asian. In choosing between the two, it all depends on your taste. The European pear tree is a real showstopper in the garden with soft fruit, while the Asian variety is crisp and juicy like an apple.

TRY THIS: Moonglow, a European variety, is a strong grower that bears flavorful fruit, but it will need to be planted with a pollinator.

7 Quince

You might be familiar with the flowering quince, but did you know you can eat the fruit? A close relative of the flowering quince, the edible quince is excellent for use in preserves, jellies and jams. In general, quinces aren't enjoyable right off the tree.

TRY THIS: It's not a shock that the Pineapple quince variety has a hint of pineapple flavor when cooked. Be sure to let quinces ripen fully on the tree before picking.

8 Orange

Did you know oranges can stay on the tree for months before you need to pick them? In some cases this even makes the fruit sweeter. If you live in the North, look for dwarf varieties that you can plant in a pot and take indoors for winter.

TRY THIS: The Trovita orange tree produces sweet fruit with outstanding flavor. A versatile grower, it's good for cooler climates but will also tolerate desert heat.

9 Plum

Plum trees are versatile, slower growers, so pruning is easy. They can handle drought, but watch out for pest problems. When buying a plum tree, make sure it's the fruiting kind, not the flowering kind.

TRY THIS: The Methley variety has purplish-red skin and a sweet taste. It ripens earlier than other varieties, so you can enjoy the plums early in the season. It's pest-resistant, too.

10 Nectarine

Nectarines are essentially peaches without the fuzz, and both types of trees require a lot of pruning, fertilizing, thinning and watering. But the flavor and juiciness of the homegrown fruit will make it all worthwhile.

TRY THIS: The supersweet Fantasia nectarine reaches peak ripeness in midseason. This variety doesn't require as much chilling as other nectarine trees, but it will still do fine in colder regions.

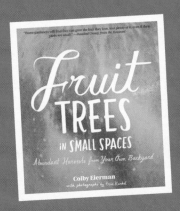

THE BASICS OF FRUIT TREE PRUNING

Pruning isn't just for looks. It's essential to the healthy growth of a tree.

It might seem like a lot of work, but by pruning your tree, you're establishing a strong framework, improving growth and encouraging flower and fruit production.

In his book *Fruit Trees in Small Spaces*, Colby Eierman talks about four types of branches you want to remove. So if you're not sure where to start pruning, look for what he calls the four D's—dead, damaged, diseased and disoriented branches. Not sure about the health of a branch? Here's a rule of thumb: If the branch drops below horizontal, it's unlikely to bear healthy fruit.

It's best to begin the pruning process in late winter, before new growth begins. But you may need to keep a close eye on fruit trees, since they sometimes need summer pruning, especially when you get some wayward branches.

gardening
for your health
health

12 ways to get growing toward a healthier lifestyle

BY DANIELLE CALKINS

Eat your vegetables! Ah, it's the ultimate mom advice that we've all heard at one point or another over the years. Don't get me wrong. It's great advice—thanks, Mom, I really do love Brussels sprouts now—but I'm starting to think the better message might be this: **Grow your vegetables!**

Think about it. If you're a gardener, chances are you care about your health. You value where your food comes from and see the importance of growing your own. But it doesn't stop there. Like many of you, I'm passionate about gardening, which naturally fits in with my love for cooking and being active.

So if you're looking for ways to incorporate healthy living into your routine, look no further than the garden! It's easy to combine cooking, gardening and being active into a happy trio that can benefit your health for years to come. Ready? Let's go!

1. START OFF SIMPLE. Growing your own vegetables is one of the best ways to kick off a healthy lifestyle. You don't have to get fancy. Even the most basic tomato plant will produce fruit that is 10 times better than what you'll get in the supermarket.

2. TRY HEIRLOOM VEGGIES. Heirlooms have been around for decades. They might not have the same commercial look as other veggies (odd-shaped tomatoes or weird colors of carrots), but they are delicious and good for you.

3. GET EXTRA VITAMINS. Did you know certain types of vegetables are healthier than others? Cue Burpee's Boost Vegetable Collection. With six varieties, it has three tomato hybrids, a pepper hybrid, a lettuce mix and a cucumber hybrid, each of them developed to provide maximum vitamins and minerals. Check them out at *burpee.com.*

4. ADD FLAVOR WITH HERBS. Something tells me you're well aware that herbs add delicious flavor to just about any meal. What you may not know is that by adding certain herbs and spices to your cooking, you gain valuable health benefits. Some herbs help protect against chronic conditions. And think about this: Adding herbs to meals is the easiest way to add flavor without a load of calories. Tempting, right?

5. ENJOY THE FRUITS OF SOMEONE ELSE'S LABOR. Maybe growing your own veggies isn't quite in the cards. Or, like me, you want to supplement your homegrown vegetables with a more diverse variety. By signing up for a community supported agriculture group (CSA), you'll be guaranteed fresh produce all summer long. Here's how it works: At the start of a growing season, you commit to either weekly or biweekly deliveries for a set price. During delivery week, expect to pick up a box of fresh farm-grown veggies.

6. GO ONLINE FOR LOCAL FLAVOR. To search for farms that offer CSAs in your area, visit *localharvest.org.* Also check out *slowfood.com,* a nonprofit member-supported association that helps educate consumers on the impact of their food choices.

7. COMMIT WITH A FRIEND. So you've decided on a CSA but are hesitant to commit. No worries. There are share sizes with everyone's needs in mind, from families to singles. If you're still feeling hesitant, grab a friend and split a share. The small sampling alone may be enough to pull you in.

8. TRY SOMETHING DIFFERENT.
I like to say the bunch of kale I got in my first CSA changed my life. It was absolutely delicious, and something I would never have considered buying on my own. Now I'm one of its biggest fans. Next time you're hesitant about a veggie, bring it home. Research it, cook with it, have fun with it. You never know what you'll end up loving.

9. EXPLORE THE FARMERS MARKET.
Wake up early on a Saturday morning and, coffee in hand or pup in tow, discover your local farmers market. It's not only a great way to mingle with neighbors, it's the perfect opportunity to pick and choose your veggies. Chat with the local farmer about why his produce is the best, and get cooking inspiration from those around you.

10. GET COOKIN'.
The beauty of vegetables, whether you prefer to grow or purchase them, is the reward that follows: enjoying them. I'll admit, I'm a healthful cook by choice, but I've come to realize that the more fresh produce I have in my fridge, the more courageous I am about experimenting with new, nutritious dishes.

11. HEAD OUTSIDE TO GET MOVING.
Cooking and gardening definitely go hand in hand, but don't forget the third component: staying active. If possible, instead of hopping in the car, walk or bike to your local farmers market. Or just make it a point to get out in your garden on a regular basis. Use our chart (at right) to determine how many calories you can burn!

12. HAVE FUN WITH IT.
What do you have to lose? Use those new, interesting veggies to spark creativity. Pair unlikely herbs with your favorite dishes; you never know what you'll come up with. And most important of all, feel good about the nutritious food you're eating.

Good luck combining gardening with an overall healthy lifestyle. The rewards are incredible. From unbeatable fresh veggies to healthier cooking, you're sure to notice a difference. I know I have.

FEEL THE BURN
The physical activity that comes with gardening is an effective way to burn calories while improving your outdoor space. Here are some of the most common gardening activities and the approximate number of calories they burn per half hour.

General gardening: 170 calories

Planting seedlings: 150 calories

Weeding a garden: 170 calories

Laying sod: 170 calories

Raking: 130 calories

Bagging leaves: 130 calories

Digging and spading dirt: 190 calories

Trimming shrubs (with a power tool): 110 calories

Mowing lawn (push mower): 210 calories

Mowing lawn (riding mower): 70 calories

Healthy Cooking pick of the month

Looking for the best healthy, in-season eats? Check out this month-by-month list of the most nutritious fruits and vegetables you can put on the table.

JANUARY: BUTTERNUT SQUASH

This fall-harvest squash wins out against its summer counterpart, zucchini, in terms of nutrition. The heart-friendly choice is low in fat and high in dietary fiber.

FEBRUARY: GARLIC

To maximize its health benefits, don't cook garlic immediately after you crush it. If you allow it to sit for 15 minutes, an enzyme reaction will boost the healthy compound it supplies.

MARCH: ASPARAGUS

Loaded with nutrients, asparagus is a good source of fiber and vitamins A, C, E and K. It's also packed with antioxidants, and research suggests it may slow the aging process.

JULY: SUMMER SQUASH

Although it's low in calories, at 36 per cup, sliced summer squash is high in nutrients. Vitamins C and A support proper function of the immune system, while magnesium will help maintain healthy bones.

AUGUST: GREEN BEANS

Also low in calories, green beans contain healthy amounts of minerals such as iron, calcium, magnesium, manganese and potassium, which are essential for metabolism.

SEPTEMBER: TOMATOES

Low in sodium and calories, tomatoes are a rich source of vitamins A, C and K. With their high water content, they can also help you feel full.

APRIL: ARTICHOKES
Artichokes have more antioxidants than any other vegetable and contain a quarter of the recommended daily intake of fiber. Bonus: Artichokes help the digestive system, too.

MAY: BELL PEPPERS
Red and green peppers are both excellent sources of vitamins C and A, as well as antioxidants that help to reduce the risk of heart disease and some cancers.

JUNE: SPINACH
Popeye shouldn't be the only fan of this leafy green. Spinach provides nearly 20 percent of the recommended daily intake of dietary fiber. The high amount of vitamin A promotes healthy skin, too.

OCTOBER: EGGPLANT
With its high fiber content and minimal calories, eggplant can help you feel full longer. Try using eggplant instead of noodles in your next pasta dish and enjoy the same size portion with just a fraction of the calories.

NOVEMBER: SWEET POTATOES
One of the healthiest vegetables around, sweet potatoes have anti-inflammatory properties and a low glycemic index, making them a good choice for diabetics.

DECEMBER: BROCCOLI
With its high potassium content, nutritious broccoli helps maintain a healthy nervous system and optimal brain function.

top
10
tasty
tomatoes

Go beyond the ordinary with these unique picks that also boast terrific flavor.

BY STACY TORNIO

1

I've grown tomatoes for as long as I can remember. Growing up, I even had my own stand at the local farmers market, selling cucumbers, peppers and lots of tomatoes. For the most part, we grew traditional red tomatoes. Every once in a while, we'd throw in a yellow or plum-shaped variety, but we didn't go off track too much.

Now I see tomatoes in a whole new light. You can find hundreds of different varieties out there in almost every hue imaginable.

To help you navigate the sea of tomatoes, we put together this Top 10 list. Of course, you'll have your own favorites, but the list is a good starting point for those who are a little overwhelmed by all the choices. And be sure to read the "Stacy's Tip" section under each pick to learn about some excellent resources for tomato and veggie fans.

1 SuperSauce

This is a new exclusive from Burpee. You wouldn't think a Roma tomato would pack such a punch, but the name really says it all. Burpee claims a single 2-pound tomato will fill an entire sauce jar. So if you like to can your own sauce, SuperSauce could be your new favorite. Just imagine what an entire plant could yield in one season.

STACY'S TIP: If you like cooking with your fruits and veggies, check out Burpee's sister company, The Cook's Garden, specializing in seeds and plants for gardening gourmets. It offers other sauce tomatoes, too. Visit *cooksgarden.com*.

2 Vernissage

You can now find a brand-new series of Vernissage tomatoes, developed by a young Ukrainian plant breeder. This pink variety with pale yellow stripes is one of the most popular, but you can grow a green, black or yellow version as well. The plants are prolific producers, and the fruit is colorful and delicious. The tomatoes average a petite 2 ounces. Just pluck them off the vine and enjoy!

STACY'S TIP: You can get Vernissage from one of our very favorite heirloom seed sources, Baker Creek Heirloom Seeds. It carries the whole Vernissage line as well as other top tomatoes. Learn more at *rareseeds.com*.

3 Casady's Folly

Have a weakness for plum tomatoes? Check out breeder Tom Wagner's creation. On the outside, each gorgeous 4-inch fruit has attractive light red and orange stripes; the interior is deep red. When you take a bite, you may notice a little bit of fruitiness. Casady's Folly will please people who like their produce in fun colors and shapes.

STACY'S TIP: We're fascinated by breeders who create new cultivars of flowers and veggies. If this interests you too, look for a new book from Timber Press, *Plant Breeding for the Home Gardener: How to Create Unique Vegetables & Flowers*. Find out more at *timberpress.com*.

1: W. ATLEE BURPEE; 2, 3: BAKER CREEK HEIRLOOM SEEDS

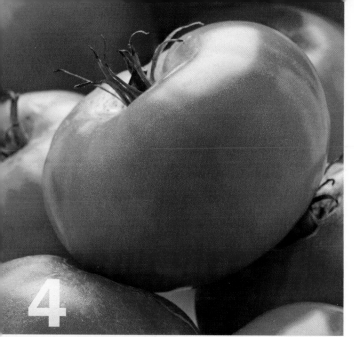

4 Grafted Brandywine

It's a fairly recent tomato trend: grafting so the plants will produce two or three times more fruit. You can find several grafted varieties, but we like the looks of the heirloom cultivar Brandywine, which has been a trusted product for decades. If you have a small space but want lots of fruit, grafted tomatoes could be the solution. Ask about them at the garden center.

STACY'S TIP: Territorial Seed Co. has a slew of grafted vegetable plants, including tomatoes such as Brandywine, Pineapple and Indigo Rose, as well as peppers and eggplants. Check out *territorialseed.com*.

5 Jasper

We pay attention to the All-America Selections each year because it's a good way to know which new flowers and veggies to watch for. In 2013, the Jasper tomato hybrid won an award in the vegetables category. At just about ¾ inch in diameter, the fruits grow in clusters and have attracted attention for superior flavor. The plant is also said to be extremely resistant to disease, which will help extend the harvest season. This is another good one to eat right off the vine.

STACY'S TIP: Following the All-America Selections each year is bound to give you inspiration for your own garden tomato choices. You can also find winners from as far back as 1979 at *all-americaselections.org*.

6 Aunt Ruby's German Green

Yes, you can do more with green tomatoes than just fry them up. While most tomatoes start green and then redden as they ripen, these are ripe when they're a vibrant lime green. The Aunt Ruby's German Green is one of the most talked-about heirlooms of the past decade. It won the Heirloom Garden Show taste test back in 2003, and many gardeners say it has better flavor than most red tomatoes.

STACY'S TIP: Another seed source worth checking out is Victory Seeds, specializing in rare, open-pollinated and heirloom garden seeds, including Aunt Ruby's. Learn more about its mission at *victoryseeds.com*.

7 Sugary

Do you know someone who doesn't like tomatoes? If so, this variety just might convert him or her. As the name suggests, it's one of the sweetest tomatoes you can grow. It also has a fun shape, pointed on both ends. A 2005 All-America Selections

4, 8, 10: W. ATLEE BURPEE; 5: ALL-AMERICAN SELECTIONS; 6: BONNIE PLANTS; 7: THE NATURAL GARDENING CO.; 9: BAKER CREEK HEIRLOOM SEEDS

winner, it's been popular ever since. It grows vigorously and will bear fruit all season, so you need only a plant or two for a good supply of fruit.

STACY'S TIP: If you prefer to purchase organic tomatoes, then be sure to check out The Natural Gardening Co. This California-based company has lots of options, including the Sugary variety. You can buy seeds or seedlings. Find out more at *naturalgardening.com*.

8 Green Zebra

What it lacks in size (only around 3 ounces), it makes up for in flavor—lots and lots of flavor. These small tomatoes fit in the palm of your hand and have lovely lime green stripes. The fruits turn yellow and soften a bit as they ripen, so you know when they're ready to pick. Chefs love having these little tomatoes on hand. And Green Bay Packers fans love how they showcase the team's colors!

STACY'S TIP: Green Zebra is an heirloom, and one of the best places to get heirlooms is through Seed Savers Exchange. This is a membership-based group, but it'll get you access to some rare and interesting seeds. Visit *seedsavers.org*.

9 Celebrity

Chances are you've seen them at your garden center. Celebrity tomatoes were an All-America Selections veggie in 1984, and we think they still deserve top honors. They're bright red, reliable and scrumptious—everything you love about tomatoes in summer. Because they've become a staple, they're readily available, making them perfect for just about any backyard.

STACY'S TIP: Many Home Depot stores sell Celebrity tomatoes. Or go to *bonnieplants.com*, which is quickly gaining recognition as a top supplier of veggies and herbs.

10 Black Cherry

Black tomatoes? Sure, as long as they taste great. And these do. They look a lot like the popular Sweet 100 cherry tomatoes, except the fruits turn from green to a deep cherry, almost black, as they ripen. This hybrid plant produces dozens of fruits on a single vine, so don't worry about sharing. You should have plenty to go around.

STACY'S TIP: Do you like black (aka "chocolate") plants? Check out one of our favorite sources for them—the Chocolate Flower Farm, *chocolateflowerfarm.com*.

FRUIT OR VEGETABLE?

Botanically, tomatoes are the fruits of the tomato plant. But in an 1893 case, Nix v. Hedden, the U.S. Supreme Court ruled that in the common language of the people, tomatoes are vegetables, just like cucumbers, beans, peas and other produce grown in home gardens. So if you want to be scientifically correct, go with fruit. If you want to keep things legal, stick with vegetable. We think they're delicious either way.

Quick Guide: Do's & Don'ts

Shopping Farmers Markets

• **DO** bring your own sturdy bag. Vendors often have bags, but you'll probably buy more than you think, so a large, heavy-duty carryall is best.

• **DON'T** be shy. The people who sell the food are probably the same ones who grow it, so ask questions, seek advice and get to know this segment of your community.

• **DO** shop outside the box. Never tried kale? Pick up a fresh bunch at the market. Or get a few apples in a variety you've never had before.

• **DON'T** eat before you go. There's more to a farmers market than fresh veggies. Local food vendors often set up shop as well. Look for bakeries or coffee shops offering sweet treats, and indulge.

• **DO** have a little bit of a plan. The market can be overwhelming when you first arrive. Know what's in season, whether it's strawberries in summer or apples in fall.

• **DON'T** expect it to be a quick trip. In general, farmers markets are leisurely, and most people peruse the goods at a relaxed pace.

Freezing Your Harvest

• **DO** blanch most vegetables before you freeze them. Blanching time will vary from just 1-2 minutes for zucchini and spinach to 7-9 minutes for artichokes.

• **DON'T** store your food in cheap plastic bags. Use freezer bags, which offer more protection.

• **DO** make sure your bags and containers are tightly sealed, and try to eliminate excess air from freezer bags. Your produce will last longer.

• **DO** use parchment paper to layer veggies such as broccoli and cauliflower in containers.

• **DON'T** forget to label. You might easily be able to tell carrots and peas from beets and beans right now, but in a few months, all bets are off. Be sure to put the date on the label, too. You'll be glad you did!

• **DON'T** freeze veggies that are too ripe or mature. You'll get best results when you freeze younger ones—small potatoes, crisp-tender peppers, young corncobs.

FREEZER TIP
For best quality, foods should be frozen in a freezer that maintains 0° and is two-thirds full.

did you know?

Learn which fruits and vegetables pack the most punch when it comes to nutrients.

1

If you had to pick the most all-around nutritious vegetable, you might say the sweet potato is No. 1. It's packed with fiber and vitamins, and it provides a healthy hit of protein, too.

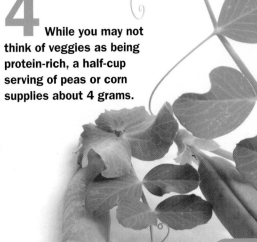

25

It's no surprise that veggies are low in calories, but did you know just how low? These top picks all have 25 calories or fewer per serving: asparagus, cucumber, celery, green beans, lettuce and summer squash.

84

Broccoli is a vitamin C powerhouse, with 84 percent of an adult's daily recommendation in a half-cup serving.

50

Everyone knows that most veggies are lower in calories than fruits are. But here are some fruits that have 50 calories or fewer per serving: strawberries, honeydew, cantaloupe, tomato and tangerine.

2.5

According to U.S. dietary guidelines, the average person should be eating 2½ cups of vegetables each day.

4

While you may not think of veggies as being protein-rich, a half-cup serving of peas or corn supplies about 4 grams.

3

Looking for a good source of vitamin A? These three veggies exceed an adult's daily recommendation in just a single serving: carrots, leaf lettuce and sweet potatoes.

BASKET: GREG SCHEIDEMANN; BROCCOLI: BRAND X PICTURES/ROBERTSTOCK; SWEET POTATOES: PHOTOSYNC/ SHUTTERSTOCK.COM; PEAS: YELLOWJ/SHUTTERSTOCK.COM; TOMATOES: SERHIY SHULLYE/SHUTTERSTOCK.COM

butterflies & Beyond

Follow monarchs as they make their journey across the border and back. Invite family and friends outdoors for a fun-filled bug hunt or moth party. Discover the plants that will bring a bevy of butterflies to your yard.

NKBIMAGES/GETTY IMAGES

THIS PAGE: ROBERT M. VERA/ALAMY; FACING PAGE: DAVE WELLING

diary of a
MONARCH

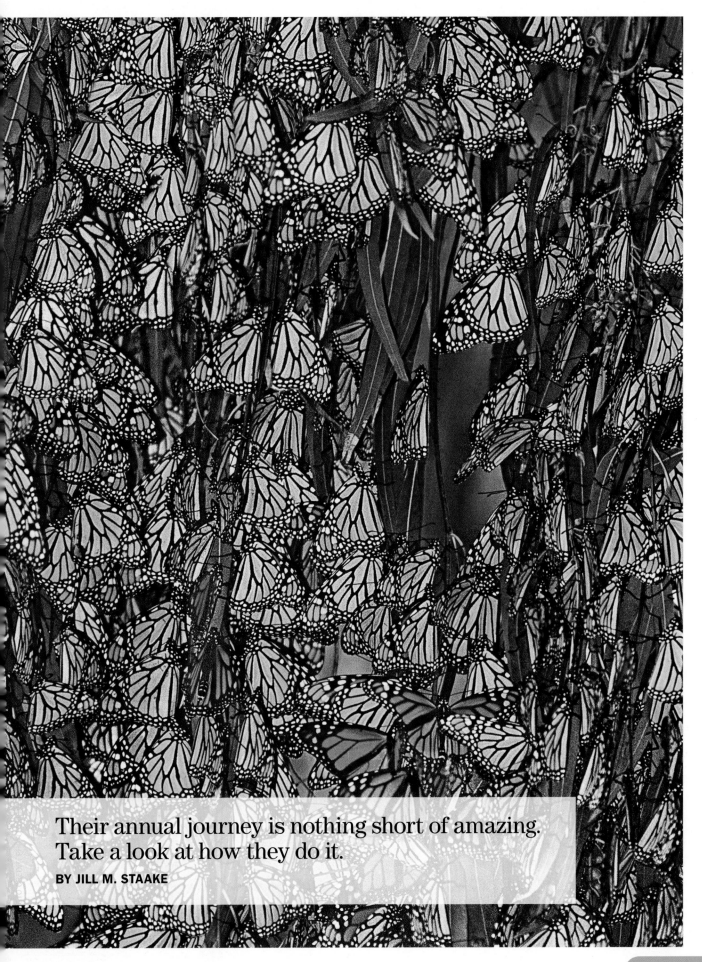

Their annual journey is nothing short of amazing.
Take a look at how they do it.

BY JILL M. STAAKE

It's an early summer morning, and an incredible new life is just beginning in the garden. It all started a few days ago, when a monarch butterfly laid an egg on a milkweed plant. The choice was no accident: Milkweed is the only food a monarch caterpillar can consume. And now this little caterpillar in Wooster, Ohio, has a job to do. Unlike other caterpillars that make a chrysalis, become butterflies and then die within a few short weeks, this one is part of the yearly "super generation." Take a look as its journey begins.

Aug. 4 ~ Wooster, Ohio

The caterpillar is about the size of a pencil point. It stays on this milkweed plant, eating and growing nonstop, leaving only if it has finished every leaf and it must find new food. Caterpillars are very hungry indeed!

Aug. 17

About two weeks have passed since the egg hatched, and the caterpillar is about 2 inches long. It crawls away from the milkweed, finding a safe and sheltered place nearby, and goes to work creating a small silk pad. It attaches itself to the pad, hanging upside down to form a "J" shape.

For 18 hours, the caterpillar is nearly motionless. Then the skin on its head suddenly splits to show a vivid green surface beneath. For several long minutes, the caterpillar wriggles, until at last the skin falls to the ground. Left behind is a soft green mass that hardens slowly into a waxy chrysalis. Now there's nothing to do but wait.

Sept. 1

The chrysalis now shows patterns of orange and black. As the first rays of sun appear, the pod cracks open and the creature's legs emerge. With effort, the rest of the body pushes out. Its crumpled wings soon straighten. The new butterfly, a female, hangs upside down, keeping still as her wings harden and dry. A couple of hours later, she flutters and flaps them, trying them out. Then the breeze catches her, and she's off into the sky for her first flight.

Sept. 30 ~ Louisville, Kentucky

As part of the super generation, this monarch has no interest in mating just yet. Instead, instincts tell her to fly fast and far. She has already flown more than 300 miles from her birthplace, and her journey has barely begun.

Oct. 10 ~ Texarkana, Texas

The monarch is now flying almost 100 miles each day, often rising a mile into the sky where strong winds easily carry her. She joins with many others of her species going in the same direction, roosting at night in trees and nectaring from asters and other late wildflowers before starting out again. The days are growing short, and there's no time to waste.

EGG: FRANCIS & JANICE BERGQUIST; CATERPILLAR ON LEAF: ROLAND JORDAHL; CHRYSALIS SERIES: ROLF NUSSBAUMER/ROLFNP.COM

Milkweed is the single most essential thing monarchs need to survive. The caterpillars can't feed on any other plant. Look for milkweed options to plant in your backyard. You can feel good that you're doing your part to keep the monarch population strong.

Help Monarchs

Over the years, it has become harder for monarchs to find the right conditions to survive and make their incredible journey. Add these to your yard to help them out:

MILKWEED It's absolutely vital to the survival of monarchs. There are more than 100 milkweed species; seek out those native to your area and plant as much as you can.

NECTAR FLOWERS Plants such as asters, cosmos, zinnias and goldenrod provide the energy migrating butterflies need in late summer and fall.

SHELTER These intrepid fliers need safe havens for rest. Shrubs and ornamental grasses are ideal. Avoid so-called "butterfly houses," which butterflies rarely use but which often attract wasps and other predators.

The transformation of monarch caterpillar to butterfly is amazing. The top photos show the process just as the butterfly is emerging. Here, monarchs prepare to roost together as they head south for their wintering grounds in Mexico.

TOP LEFT: FRANCIS & JANICE BERGQUIST; REMAINING PHOTOS: DAYBREAK IMAGERY

Oct. 17 ~ Ciudad Acuna, Mexico

Two months after leaving her birthplace, the monarch crosses into Mexico and joins millions of others to make clouds of orange in the blue sky. Her wings show some wear and tear but beat faithfully, carrying her on without stopping. Soon enough, she'll have plenty of time to rest.

Nov. 2 ~ El Rosario winter colony, Michoacan, Mexico

Finally, she has reached the wintering grounds. It's surprisingly cool here in the mountains, 10,000 feet above sea level. She settles with other monarchs into the oyamel fir trees, so thick with the creatures that branches sometimes crack from the weight. The insects' bodies shut down, a type of hibernation known as torpor.

Dec. 30

Last night a terrible storm swept through the colony, with pounding rains, treacherous winds and freezing temperatures. This morning the ground beneath the trees is littered with the tattered bodies of butterflies that did not survive. Our monarch, however, is safe in her sheltered perch close to the tree trunk. She stirs briefly in the morning sun, then is still once more.

Feb. 23

Days are longer now, and the sun is stronger. High in the trees, the monarch begins to stir. Suddenly, she and others leave the trees, filling the air with a blur of orange and black. After months of near silence in the grove, the sound of flapping wings is unbelievably loud. The insects spread their wings in the warm sun and sip water from wet rocks. They won't stay long, though; there is no food for them here, nor milkweed on which to lay eggs. They must start back north again, retracing their fall path.

March 15 ~ Abilene, Texas

Here in Texas, spring wildflowers are in bloom, and our female feeds on columbine while a male flutters nearby. After many months and thousands of miles, she is at last ready to mate. The two butterflies dance in the air and then join together. In a few days, she will begin to lay her hundreds of eggs on newly emerged milkweed plants. Her offspring and their offspring will complete the flight back to Ohio and beyond over several generations, each living only about six weeks. In the fall, another super generation will be born.

March 29 ~ Wichita Falls, Texas

She has laid all her eggs; it is her final task. Her wings are battered and ragged at the edges, faded and pale. Her body and wings are still, stirred only by a sweet spring breeze. The same gentle wind ruffles a milkweed leaf nearby, where a tiny caterpillar has just crawled from its egg. It raises its head to the sun, and the cycle begins anew.

watching
butterflies

They're as pretty as confetti in
the sky—but if you know where
to look, you can marvel at their
delicate beauty up close.

BY KEN KEFFER

You don't have to be a scientist to enjoy watching
butterflies. (By the way, did you know that people
who study them are called lepidopterists?) Butterfly
watching has caught on as a hobby in recent
decades, and it's not hard to see why. You don't have
to spend much time in the backyard before you'll
notice them flitting about. And with more than
650 species in the U.S. alone, there's a good chance
you'll see something new and interesting.

Julia heliconian
butterfly

For tips and advice, we consulted lepidopterist Robert Michael Pyle. The author of the *National Audubon Society Field Guide to North American Butterflies*, he did a Big Year of butterfly watching in 2008, setting out to see as many species as possible in 365 days—and writing another book, *Mariposa Road*, about the adventures of seeing all of the different species.

But you don't have to devote a whole year to chasing butterflies to enjoy them. By simply slowing down, you'll start to notice these beauties all around you. As Pyle says, it's as easy as "visiting any sunny, flowery spot, standing still and seeing what happens."

The Essentials

Good news! You don't have to wake up with the birds to see butterflies. In fact, brunch time might be your best shot at peak diversity. Different species are active at different hours, so you can be in a single spot all day long and always find something new and intriguing.

One trick is to watch for specialized behavior such as basking and hilltopping. Especially on chilly mornings, butterflies can be found sunbathing, or basking, with their wings spread or folded flat so the warm rays elevate their body temperature. Swallowtails and some other species often gather in large numbers for hilltopping: Males cluster on open hilltops, while females look for suitable mates before flying downhill to seek host plants for laying eggs.

Fiery skipper

Dorcas copper

You could see groups of monarchs like these during migration season as they fly south.

SKIPPER: DAVE WELLING; DORCAS COPPER: CAROL L. EDWARDS; MONARCHS: DOUG WECHSLER; FEEDER, PAINTED LADY: DAYBREAK IMAGERY

Make your own butterfly feeder by offering rotting fruit.

Painted lady

Learn how to get involved in official butterfly counts through the North American Butterfly Association, *naba.org.*

Discover the Locals

Do a little research about the species in your area. The North American Butterfly Association is a great resource; local chapters offer numerous field trips as well. Some state wildlife agencies can also provide valuable information about local butterflies.

Most butterflies are choosy about habitat while some are more widespread. A field guide will help you with identification and ranges. Many species look quite similar, but learning the major characteristics of butterfly families will help you figure out what's what. One thing you'll never have to worry about, of course, is identifying a butterfly by its song.

Bring Them to You

Almost any garden will attract certain species, but why not do some planning and plant a full-scale butterfly garden, with nectar plants to feed adults and plants to nourish caterpillars?

Or set up a feeding station by putting out fruit, especially citrus and rotting bananas.

Seeing a butterfly proboscis in action is fascinating; I've spent hours watching eastern commas at my small window-tray feeder.

Simply watering the ground will attract butterflies, too: They'll gather the salt they need from the edges of mud puddles. I've seen many a butterfly do this on hiking trails after a rain, but your backyard can be just as welcome an oasis.

Flight of the Butterfly

Learn a little about flight periods. The adults of some species are visible for just a few weeks or even a few days a year. Pyle says that "in a given place you will generally find different suites of butterflies on the wing in early spring, midsummer and early autumn." Some species have a single brood each season, while others produce multiple generations in that time, resulting in extended flight periods with distinct peaks during the year.

Most species overwinter as eggs, caterpillars or chrysalises. Don't give up on butterflies in the

Make butterfly watching

fun by seeing how many butterflies you can spot in one day or one weekend.

Dusky blue
hairstreak

Where to Go Butterfly Watching

Many species are abundant and widespread, but some can be found only in small areas. Author Robert Michael Pyle racked up more than 87,700 miles during his Big Year adventure to see butterflies, including more than 32,500 miles in Powdermilk, his 1982 Honda Civic hatchback. Here are some of Pyle's favorite destinations for butterfly watching:

- North Slope, Alaska
- Sky Islands, Arizona
- Sierra Nevada, California
- Alpine Mountains, Colorado
- Everglades National Park and Florida Keys, Florida
- Ozark Mountains, Missouri
- Pine Barrens, New Jersey
- Lower Rio Grande Valley and Big Bend, Texas
- Prairie remnants throughout the Midwest

You could go the traditional route and catch butterflies, such as the tiger swallowtail at left, in a net. Or look for a group of butterflies, like the sulphurs below, gathering at mud puddles.

winter, though. Mourning cloaks, commas and a few other species can be seen on the wing on warm winter days.

Photography and Optics

Both digital cameras and close-focusing binoculars have reduced the frustration of many butterfly watchers. "It still takes care and stealth to approach your subject, but with luck, patience and practice, you can obtain near views of many of the butterflies and other insects you encounter," Pyle says.

One approach is to remain still and let them come to you. Challenge yourself to observe a single section of your flower bed. Take note of the behavior of different butterflies. Did they tend to visit the same plants again and again? How many kinds of butterflies did you spot in an hour?

Butterfly Nets

Using a net is one of the cheapest and most effective ways to see butterflies. It's fun, too! Catching butterflies in a net is pure joy for young and old alike. Once you have a flier in sight, an easy catch-and-release can satisfy your curiosity. If you're more of a hands-on person, be quick and extremely gentle when you examine your catch, making sure to release it unharmed.

Whether you're a casual observer or the next Robert Michael Pyle, take a moment to appreciate these backyard beauties. The more butterflies you see, the more you'll want to learn about these amazing creatures. Perhaps you're a bit more of a lepidopterist than you imagined.

do you know your state butterfly?

OREGON
Oregon Swallowtail

MONTANA
Mourning Cloak

IDAHO
Monarch

MINNESO[T]A
Monar[ch]

CALIFORNIA
California Dogface

COLORADO
Colorado Hairstreak

ARIZONA
Two-Tailed Swallowtail

NEW MEXICO
Sandia Hairstreak

OKLAHOMA
Black Swallowtail

TEXAS
Monarch

HAWAII
Pulelehua

Love Butterflies?
Our friends at **Gardens With Wings** provided this list for us. For helpful tips on attracting butterflies near you, check out *gardenswithwings.com*.

Take a minute to learn about these honored representatives.

Many people know their state bird and flower, but their state butterfly? Who knew that was even a thing? Actually, in most cases, they're officially state insects, but just take a look at this wide butterfly representation.

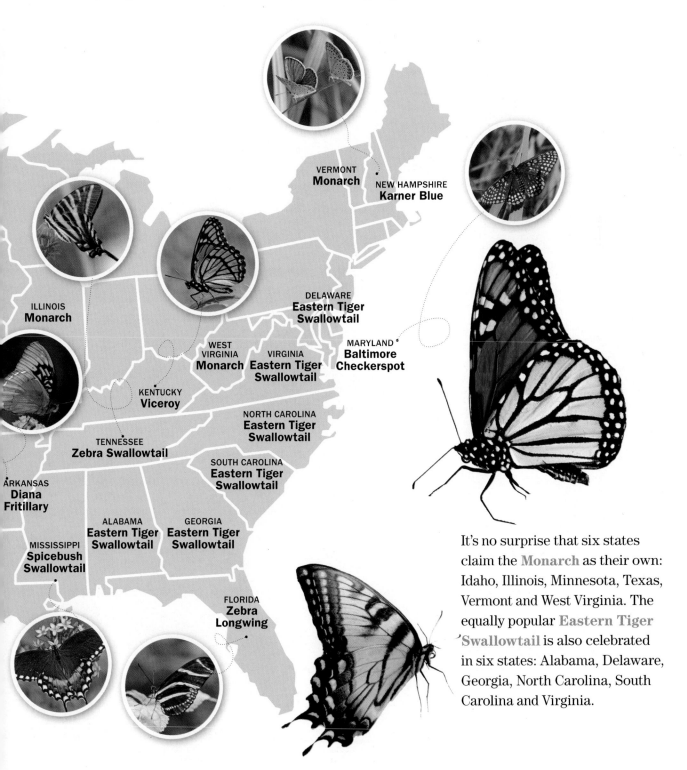

VERMONT
Monarch

NEW HAMPSHIRE
Karner Blue

ILLINOIS
Monarch

DELAWARE
Eastern Tiger Swallowtail

WEST VIRGINIA
Monarch

VIRGINIA
Eastern Tiger Swallowtail

MARYLAND
Baltimore Checkerspot

KENTUCKY
Viceroy

NORTH CAROLINA
Eastern Tiger Swallowtail

TENNESSEE
Zebra Swallowtail

SOUTH CAROLINA
Eastern Tiger Swallowtail

ARKANSAS
Diana Fritillary

ALABAMA
Eastern Tiger Swallowtail

GEORGIA
Eastern Tiger Swallowtail

MISSISSIPPI
Spicebush Swallowtail

FLORIDA
Zebra Longwing

It's no surprise that six states claim the Monarch as their own: Idaho, Illinois, Minnesota, Texas, Vermont and West Virginia. The equally popular Eastern Tiger Swallowtail is also celebrated in six states: Alabama, Delaware, Georgia, North Carolina, South Carolina and Virginia.

Here, spicebush and pipevine swallowtails feed on butterfly weed, one of the most popular blooms for attracting many different kinds of butterflies. At right, a Reakirt's blue butterfly perches on a flower bud.

Year-round
BUTTERFLY GUIDE

Here's what to look for as the habits of these irresistible charmers change with the seasons.

BY KENN KAUFMAN

Summer is peak butterfly season with warm, sunny weather that sends colorful sulphurs, monarchs and swallowtails flitting through our gardens. But you might be surprised to know that there's significant butterfly activity in every season. Take a look at what you might expect to see throughout the year.

Spring: Welcome, Butterflies

In the southernmost U.S., winter fades almost imperceptibly into spring. Elsewhere, however, particular species are sure signs of springtime. Among these are small white butterflies like West Virginia and spring whites, and various types of orangetips and marbles. Their caterpillars feed on wild plants in the mustard family, which grow mainly in spring. The adult butterflies must emerge early so females can lay eggs and the caterpillars can feed while the plants are available.

Other spring specialties include certain tiny blue butterflies, such as the spring azure and the silvery blue. These gems may show up in gardens or gather by the dozens around the edges of mud puddles. Less noticeable are some small, dark hairstreaks and skippers—somewhat obscure, but worth seeking out for their poetic names, like frosted elfin and sleepy duskywing. But no one is likely to overlook some of the big swallowtails that start flying early in the season, such as the gorgeous streamer-winged zebra swallowtail.

Early in spring, monarchs that have wintered in Mexico begin to move north. A few others—red admirals, painted ladies and American ladies among them—are on the move, too. In the Southwest, tens of thousands of painted ladies may join in a mass flight, flooding into gardens along their path.

Week by week, new nonmigratory species emerge. Bright sulphurs, subtle satyrs, flashy fritillaries and others add to the gorgeous color palette that will grace summer yards and gardens.

The painted lady butterfly is found throughout North America and looks very similar to the American lady.

Common buckeyes (above) are a popular and common butterfly in summer because they will sit out in the open, often on bare ground.

PAINTED LADY: DENNIS STROMBERG; BUCKEYE: PIECEOFLACE

Summer: Beauty at Its Peak

A large and diverse garden is often alive with butterflies all summer long. Casual observers may think they're seeing the same ones over and over, but the reality is more complicated and more interesting.

Most adult butterflies live two to three weeks at most. With common small species like pearl crescents and tailed blues, the first females to emerge in spring or early summer lay eggs that will soon hatch. The caterpillars will grow rapidly and pupate, and another batch of adults will appear; there may be three or more generations in the warm months.

Shorter summers often mean fewer generations. Several species, including some of the swallowtails, may have several broods a year in the Deep South but only one in the North. And some, including the great spangled fritillary, have a single generation each year regardless of latitude.

Of course, summer is also when many migratory southern species push northward. Tropical sulphurs and skippers fly from Mexico into the American Southwest; widespread butterflies such as buckeyes and red admirals may reach up beyond the Great Lakes. By summer's end, migratory monarchs have reached the northern U.S. and far into Canada, poised for the temperature drop that will send them drifting south again.

In Alaska and Arctic Canada, a few butterflies—mostly lesser fritillaries and satyrs—fly only every other year. Summers are so short that the caterpillars hatch in one season, hibernate through one winter, feed and grow through the following summer, and then hibernate through a second winter before pupating and emerging as adults in their second summer. That's why a species can be common one summer and seemingly nowhere to be found the next.

Fall: Winding Down

Most adult butterflies will perish before winter arrives. Long before the intense cold sets in, the females will have laid eggs, ensuring a new generation for the next year.

With that taken care of, the adults may spend the rest of their short lives wandering in a seemingly aimless way. But some species do live through the winter, hibernating in sheltered sites, and they may be seeking out these roosting spots as fall advances. Mourning cloaks, question marks, commas and tortoiseshells are among these hibernators, so if you see them flitting about woodpiles or tree cavities in fall, they are likely looking for winter shelter.

A few varieties fly only in late summer and fall. The red-bordered satyr, which makes its rather floppy way through Southwestern canyons in September, is one; another is Leonard's skipper, a denizen of Northeastern meadows. Few of these appear in gardens, however; most of what you'll see in your backyard is a continuation of summer habits, like the northern push of southern species. Subtropical creatures like big pale cloudless sulphurs and tiny orange fiery skippers may still be heading north in early October, even filtering into southern Canada.

Butterfly ID Tips

Grab a field guide and ask yourself these questions when you see an unfamiliar butterfly:

SIZE How many inches is the wingspan?
SHAPE Is there a tail? Are the wings jagged or scalloped?
POSTURE How is it sitting? Wings folded up tight, spread wide, or half open in a V shape?
FLIGHT STYLE Is it flying with steady flaps, a quick flutter or completely erratically?
FIELD MARKS Is there a spot of color?

Comma butterflies (such as the one above) will look for a place to hibernate for winter.

Red admiral

Mourning cloak

Winter: Hiding Out

Along the Gulf of Mexico, in the lowlands of the desert Southwest and on California's coast, mild winters allow some butterflies to keep flying. They may be out of sight on cool, cloudy days, but red admirals, painted ladies and others fly in warmth.

East of the Rockies, most monarchs are absent, having flown to Mexico. But much of the Western population spends the season in coastal California. They are sedentary, hanging in dense clusters in tall trees. On warm days, they'll scatter to the wind like orange and black confetti, drifting back to the roost as evening nears.

Relatively few other species migrate, surviving the cold months in any of their four major life stages.

A few tough butterflies hibernate as adults; a February thaw may wake them, producing the startling sight of a mourning cloak, comma or tortoiseshell fluttering over lingering snowdrifts. Some swallowtails and others spend the winter as pupae, ready to emerge as adults in spring. Still others overwinter in the egg stage.

Caterpillars might seem more vulnerable, but the majority of our butterflies spend the winter in that form. They may even hatch out of the egg in fall and not begin to eat until spring. So even when northern regions are locked in ice and snow, next summer's butterflies take the shape of myriad tiny caterpillars sleeping in the cold.

top
10
host plants

Garden for butterflies at the next level—
provide food for hungry caterpillars.

BY KIRSTEN SWEET

White peacock
butterfly

1

Nectar plants give butterfly gardens a powerful boost. But they're not the only key to drawing pretty pollinators to your yard. As your favorite winged beauties transition through their life cycle, many lay eggs on the undersides of specific plants—hosts. Many people know monarchs need milkweed, but there are a number of other host plants you should consider adding to your garden. By incorporating some of these, you'll attract a wider variety of butterflies to your backyard. And now they just might stick around!

1 Passionflower

Passiflora, Zones 5 to 9

Passionflower is a perfect butterfly-friendly vine. It climbs 15 to 50 feet and will thrive in full sun or part shade. If you're starting this beauty from seed or small nursery plants, be prepared to provide support for its tendrils to cling and wind. After that, you won't need to put in much effort to enjoy the blooms of this climber.

BUTTERFLY BENEFITS: Several fritillary caterpillars mow down on passionflower. A couple of common ones are the gulf fritillary and the variegated fritillary.

2 Hollyhock

Alcea rosea, Zones 2 to 10

If you want to make an impact in your garden, this tall host plant is an easy choice. It comes in many colors, attracts an array of insects and can reach up to 8 feet in height. Plant hollyhocks in full sun and along a fence or wall for stability.

BUTTERFLY BENEFITS: Painted lady caterpillars rely on several different plants as food sources, including hollyhocks and various spring annuals.

3 Willow

Salix, Zones 2 to 9

It's true! Caterpillars feed on trees as well as pretty garden plants. Willows are known to grow up to 100 feet depending on species. So most gardeners will want smaller willows, like Dappled or Flame willow, which are a better size for backyard landscapes. Willow trees prefer full sun and tolerate many soil types.

BUTTERFLY BENEFITS: Several caterpillars like to munch on willow trees, including viceroy, western tiger swallowtail and mourning cloak.

4 Dill

Anethum graveolens, annual

Generally grown for its culinary uses, dill is also an unconventionally attractive garden plant with its feathery, aromatic green leaves and yellow buds. For an herb plant, dill gets quite large, reaching up to 4 feet tall.

BUTTERFLY BENEFITS: If you're looking to snip some dill for use in your own kitchen, you've got to get your hands on it before the black swallowtails chow down. Anise swallowtails and other caterpillars like dill as well.

5 Chokecherry

Prunus virginiana, Zones 2 to 6

In spring, long bloom clusters appear in a stunning display on the branches of chokecherry trees. Later in the season, the tree produces berries perfect for birds to munch on. This tree grows about 30 feet tall, so be sure to leave plenty of space for this beauty to mature.

BUTTERFLY BENEFITS: A western species, the two-tailed swallowtail caterpillar, enjoys feeding on the foliage of the chokecherry tree.

6 Snapdragon

Antirrhinum majus, annual

Mostly grown as an annual or a short-lived perennial in Zones 5 to 9, snapdragons are great for adding height to a landscape. These garden classics' stalks can reach about 4 feet tall with blooms in a variety of colors: white, pink, purple, orange or red.

BUTTERFLY BENEFITS: Look for common buckeye caterpillars snacking away on your snapdragons. They're fun butterflies to have in your yard because they're easily identifiable by bold, colorful eyespots.

7 Violet

Viola, Zones 3 to 10

If you've got partial shade, try this pretty option. Perennial violets bloom in spring and prefer partial shade, while annual violas actually prefer full sun but will thrive in the cooler temperatures of partial shade. They're dainty plants with a maximum height of only about 6 inches.

BUTTERFLY BENEFITS: Violets are the host plants for the widespread great spangled fritillary, as well as western fritillaries like Mormon, callippe and zerene.

8 Oak

Quercus, Zones 3 to 10

You may know oak trees by the fantastic orange, red and yellow color show they put on every autumn. Mature oaks can reach up to 100 feet high, but you can find smaller varieties, such as pin oak, that grow to about 75 feet—still quite large. So keep in mind that even smaller varieties need plenty of space to grow and flourish.

BUTTERFLY BENEFITS: Young oak leaves are favorites of the caterpillars of Horace's duskywing and banded hairstreak.

9 Everlasting

Anaphalis margaritacea, Zones 3 to 8

Maybe you're more familiar with this plant by the common name pearly everlasting, but its beauty is the same no matter what you call it. Blooming from midsummer to early fall, this plant boasts small, flat-topped clumps of white flowers reaching about 2 feet tall.

BUTTERFLY BENEFITS: American lady butterflies can be found throughout most of the United States, so plant everlasting to feed those hungry caterpillars.

10 Switchgrass

Panicum virgatum, Zones 4 to 9

This easygoing and versatile grass is a good choice for wet conditions, drought or partial shade, as long as it's planted in moist, well-draining soil. Growing narrow and upright with a cloud of seed heads in fall, switchgrass can reach more than 5 feet tall. Birds enjoy the seeds while the green leaves turn to yellow in fall.

BUTTERFLY BENEFITS: Many skipper caterpillars need grasses like switchgrass as a food source. The same caterpillars might overwinter on or underneath the blades of grass.

More Plants for Butterflies
...and the fliers they attract

ASTER cabbage white, common buckeye, red admiral

BLACK-EYED SUSAN great spangled fritillary, American snout, silvery checkerspot

CONEFLOWERS giant swallowtail, pearl crescent, painted lady

BUTTERFLY WEED Eastern tiger swallowtail, coral hairstreak, American copper

SUNFLOWER American lady, spicebush swallowtail, wild indigo duskywing

Halloween pennant

appreciating dragonflies

Find out why you should want these
gossamer-winged insects in your yard.

PHOTOS AND STORY BY BILL JOHNSON

You probably encounter them every
summer. They're hard to miss, with
their large wings, bright colors and
quick movements as they dart here
and there, feasting on a hapless
mosquito or an errant fly. They're the
dragonflies.

As a bug, butterfly and overall
insect enthusiast, I find that people
know fairly little about dragonflies.
Sure, they're pretty and have a cool
name, but what else should you know
about these abundant fliers? Let me
have the honor of introducing you to
this wonderful group of insects.

Friends in the Backyard

Consider dragonflies your allies.
They're good to have around
because they help control pests like
mosquitoes, flies and other flying

Have you ever seen dragonflies stick their tails up in the air? It's called "obelisking," and they do it on hot summer days to reduce their exposure to the sun's rays.

Blue dasher

Eastern amberwing

Bluet damselfly

So what's the difference between a dragonfly and a damselfly? Though they share many similarities, they belong to different scientific suborders. For a quick way to tell the difference, look at the way one holds its wings at rest. If the wings are out, parallel to the ground, you're looking at a dragonfly. If the wings are pressed together (left), it's a damselfly.

insects. A single dragonfly can eat its own weight in smaller insects in just 30 minutes.

The U.S. is home to more than 400 dragonfly species belonging to 11 families. Within those families are groups informally known by such names as meadowhawks, clubtails, darners, emeralds and skimmers.

Some species have forbidding nicknames, like devil's darning needles, snake feeders and horse stingers. But don't be fooled: These names are usually based on folklore. Dragonflies are completely harmless to humans.

Impressive From the Beginning

Dragonflies begin their lives underwater. The immature form, known as a naiad, is able to breathe underwater by the use of gills similar to those of a fish. When the naiad is fully grown, it will crawl out of the water, usually up a stick or a reed, into the air, where the exoskeleton will split open and an adult dragonfly will emerge. The adult rests for a bit, pumping blood into its wings. At first the wing movement is flimsy and fragile, but eventually the wings become rigid.

Several things make dragonflies the accurate and powerful hunters they are. With two large eyes that wrap around most of the head, their vision is excellent. The eyes have more than 30,000 facets, giving them close to a 360-degree field of vision.

Dragonflies are also spectacular fliers. Not only can they reach speeds

of up to 45 miles an hour, they can also cruise very slowly, stop and hover. They can even back up in midair.

Just sitting and watching them can be entertaining. As hunters, they commonly work from a perch, which can become their territorial home base as well as their launching pad for going after prey. If you quietly, patiently observe them, you'll see them leave the perch, dart around and most likely return to the same perch.

The presence of dragonflies is always a good sign for the health of the environment around them. So welcome them to your yard!

Luna moth resting on blue delphinium

throw a moth party

Gather a few lights,
bring some bananas
and invite friends for
a little late-night fun.

BY KENN AND KIMBERLY KAUFMAN

Tiger moth

We all love the way butterflies lure us into the garden by day, but the magic doesn't have to end when the sun goes down. Along with butterflies, moths belong to the order lepidoptera. When the light leaves the sky and the butterflies go to sleep, the late-night lepidoptera come out to play! Butterflies get all the press, but the popularity of moth watching is growing, and with good reason. If you still think of moths as drab little things that eat your sweaters, their beauty and diversity will amaze you.

With 11,000 species in the U.S. and Canada (compared with only about 700 species of butterflies), moths are everywhere. They also come in a dizzying array of sizes and patterns, in colors ranging from subtle to dazzling. Once you start paying attention, you'll see why moth watching is an endless source of learning and fun.

Attracting Moths: Lights, Sheet, Bait, Action!

Simply leaving your porch light on will attract a few moths, but you can increase your chances of finding impressive ones by following some simple tips.

We started "mothing" together a few years ago, and it was so much fun that we decided to share the excitement with our friends. In recent years we've been hosting moth parties—and you can do the same in your backyard! Here are some pointers.

Crucial Equipment

Although the precise reason remains uncertain, most moths are attracted to artificial lights. Serious moth watchers sometimes use very elaborate setups, even taking generators way out into the woods, but you don't have to go to such lengths.

At our house, the porch light isn't in the best position for visibility, so we run an extension cord out into the backyard and hang a couple of lights on an old camera tripod. One is a bright white light; the other is a black (ultraviolet) light that emits a pale blue glow. You can find inexpensive black lights at hardware stores or even party-supply stores. Some moths are more attracted to black lights than to standard ones, so using both kinds can dramatically increase the number and the diversity of moths you'll see.

The Backdrop

Next, we hang a plain white sheet right behind the black light. The cheapest quality will do; the sheet is there for the moths to land on and to make it easier for you to see and photograph them. You can hang the sheet from a clothesline or a rope tied between two trees, or tack it to the side of a building. It's also a good idea to put another white sheet on the ground under the lights, so you can see underfoot and avoid stepping on any of your little guests.

Reel 'Em In

Unlike their fellow winged creatures, some moths aren't particularly attracted to lights. Fortunately, there's another lure you can use: bait! Here's the simple recipe that works best for us. In a large wide-mouthed container, mix five or six really overripe bananas (so far gone that the peels are black), 2 pounds of brown sugar and 20 ounces of cheap

If you still think of moths as drab little things that eat your sweaters, their beauty and diversity will amaze you.

Cecropia moth

Girlfriend underwing moth

beer. Stir the mixture until it's well-blended. The bait works best if you prepare it in advance and let it ferment for a few days before using it, but you don't have to.

To use, take a wide paintbrush and simply spread the mixture onto the bark of a tree—or several trees—at eye level. A spot about a foot square should do. Moths will detect the scent of the bait and come to feast on your sugary offering. Using a flashlight, check the bait as often as you like to see who's coming by. If you watch closely, you may be able to see a moth's long, slender, tonguelike proboscis as it sips the bait.

Many other insects—colorful little beetles at the bait, dainty mayflies at the lights—may be attracted to your moth offerings, too. All are fascinating to watch. Just keep an open mind and enjoy your discoveries.

It's Better With Friends

Lights, sheets and bait are essential, but don't forget the human guests. Moth watching on your own is fun and interesting, but you'll amplify the excitement when friends share the experience. Moths are captivating to children in particular. What kid wouldn't love playing outside after dark with flashlights and staying up past bedtime?

It's a marvelous thing when you discover that adventures in nature can happen under the stars as well as in sunlight. We hope you'll host your own moth party and explore the late-night lepidoptera in your yard!

Geometer moth caterpillar

This sphinx moth is feeding on bergamot. One of the few daytime moths, it is often mistaken for a hummingbird.

MOTH GROUPS

Identifying all 11,000 species of North American moths would be a monumental challenge, but some basic groups are easy to recognize.

SILK MOTHS: This group includes our largest moths, such as the beautiful pale green luna and the huge polyphemus. Adults live for only a few days and, remarkably, do not feed at all, so you may attract them with lights but not bait.

SPHINX MOTHS: These strong, fast fliers can be seen hovering at flowers the way hummingbirds do. At rest, they look like little fighter jets poised for takeoff.

GEOMETER MOTHS: Appearing in all colors and patterns, they usually rest with their wings stretched straight out to the sides, and they often have stripes that continue across all four wings. Their caterpillars are the little inchworms we see looping their way across leaves and twigs.

UNDERWING MOTHS: Members of this group are often much more attracted to bait than to lights. Their forewings are dull and camouflaged, but their hindwings have bright, colorful patterns.

Polyphemus moth

Praying mantis

go on a
bug hunt

Look for nature's tiny creatures in your own backyard.

BY DAVID MIZEJEWSKI

Some of the coolest animals on the planet don't have fur or feathers or four legs. Insects, spiders and other invertebrates are all around, living out the daily drama of predator and prey just outside your door. They might be smaller and more common, but they're no less exciting than larger, more elusive animals. You can enjoy miniature wildlife and relive your childhood by going on a bug hunt in your own garden.

It's as simple as grabbing a butterfly net, a magnifying glass, a field guide and a jar with holes poked in the lid. Head to the garden and see what critters await. Catch them with the net and put them in the jar, or simply scoop them up. Get a closer look with the magnifying glass and try

PRAYING MANTIS, LADYBUG: ROLF NUSSBAUMER/ROLFNPCOM; CATERPILLAR: DAVE WELLING; SPIDER: NANISIMOVA/SHUTTERSTOCK.COM

Seven-spotted ladybug

Argiope spider

Have kids or grandkids? A bug hunt is sure to get them excited about nature. They might even learn something, too!

Monarch caterpillar

to identify your catch with the field guide. Many species are delicate, so handle them carefully and release them where you caught them. You'll be surprised at how a little knowledge will take away the "ick" factor.

Here are some of the easiest species to spot and catch:

Ladybugs

Most ladybug species are bright red with black spots, but some are orange, mostly black or even spotless. Look for them on herbaceous plants, where they hang out devouring aphids. Their larvae, shaped like alligator heads, are no less interesting—or predatory.

Fireflies

These beetles have species-specific flash patterns, which they use to find mates. They're also important predators of soft-bodied garden pests, including slugs. Nothing says childhood fun like a glass jar full of these magical insects glowing on a summer evening.

Spiders

Not all spiders catch their meals in sticky webs. Some chase their prey down or ambush and pounce on it. Large argiope spiders actually weave a zigzag into their webs to alert larger animals so they don't walk or fly through the delicate mesh. In early autumn, you can spot ground-hunting wolf spiders at night by shining a flashlight on the ground and looking for their glowing eyes.

Caterpillars

Just as diverse in appearance as they are in their butterfly stage, caterpillars are fun to observe. Some feature psychedelic stripes, some have fake "eyes" to ward off predators, while others are camouflaged to look like bird droppings (yuck!).

Mantids

Praying mantises are great garden predators. Their large size can be intimidating, but their alien appearance is one of the most amazing in the animal kingdom. This fall, look for their inch-long egg cases attached to branches. The case protects the eggs through the winter and, come spring, opens to release hundreds of miniature replicas of the adults.

Tiger swallowtail on jupiter's beard
Photo by Mark Turner/Turner Photographics

Common buckeye
Finalist in our Backyard Photo Contest
Photo by James Burns

Monarchs on sunflower
Finalist in our Backyard Photo Contest
Photo by Patty Jennings

Gray hairstreak
Finalist in our Backyard Photo Contest
Photo by Michael McCaffrey

Cecropia moth
Finalist in our Backyard Photo Contest
Photo by Janice Perry

Birdhouse Guidelines

Discover which dwellings are best for your backyard birds.

SPECIES	DIMENSIONS	HOLE	PLACEMENT	COLOR	NOTES
Eastern bluebird	5" x 5" x 8"h.	$1\frac{1}{2}$" centered 6" above floor	5-10' high in the open; sunny area	light earth tones	likes open areas, especially facing a field
Tree swallow	5" x 5" x 6"h.	1" centered 4" above floor	5-8' high in the open; 50-100% sun	light earth tones or gray	within 2 miles of pond or lake
Purple martin	multiple apts. 6" x 6" x 6" ea. (minimum)	$2\frac{1}{8}$" hole $2\frac{1}{4}$" above floor	15-20' high in the open	white	open yard without tall trees; near water
Tufted titmouse	4" x 4" x 8"h.	$1\frac{1}{4}$"	4-10' high	light earth tones	prefers to live in or near woods
Chickadee	4" x 4" x 8"h. or 5" x 5" base	$1\frac{1}{8}$" centered 6" above floor	4-8' high	light earth tones	small tree thicket
Nuthatch	4" x 4" x 10"h.	$1\frac{1}{4}$" centered $7\frac{1}{2}$" above floor	12-25' high on tree trunk	bark-covered or natural	prefers to live in or near woods
House wren	4" x 4" x 8"h. or 4" x 6" base	1" centered 6" above floor	5-10' high on post or hung in tree	light earth tones or white	prefers lower branches of backyard trees
Northern flicker	7" x 7" x 18"h.	$2\frac{1}{2}$" centered 14" above floor	8-20' high	light earth tones	put 4" sawdust inside for nesting
Downy woodpecker	4" x 4" x 10"h.	$1\frac{1}{4}$" centered $7\frac{1}{2}$" above floor	12-25' high on tree trunk	simulate natural cavity	prefers own excavation; provide sawdust
Red-headed woodpecker	6" x 6" x 15"h.	2" centered 6-8" above floor	8-20' high on post or tree trunk	simulate natural cavity	needs sawdust for nesting
Wood duck	10" x 10" x 24"h.	4" x 3" elliptical 20" above floor	2-5' high on post over water, or 12-40' high on tree facing water	light earth tones or natural	needs 3-4" of sawdust or shavings for nesting
American kestrel	10" x 10" x 24"h.	4" x 3" elliptical 20" above floor	12-40' high on post or tree trunk	light earth tones or natural	needs open approach on edge of woodlot or in isolated tree
Screech-owl	10" x 10" x 24"h.	4" x 3" elliptical 20" above floor	12-40' high on tree	light earth tones or natural	prefers open woods or edge of woodlot

Note: With the exception of wrens and purple martins, birds do not tolerate swaying birdhouses. Birdhouses should be firmly anchored to a post, a tree or the side of a building.

Source: *Garden Birds of America* by George H. Harrison. Willow Creek Press, 1996.

What's Your Zone?
Plant Hardiness Zone Map

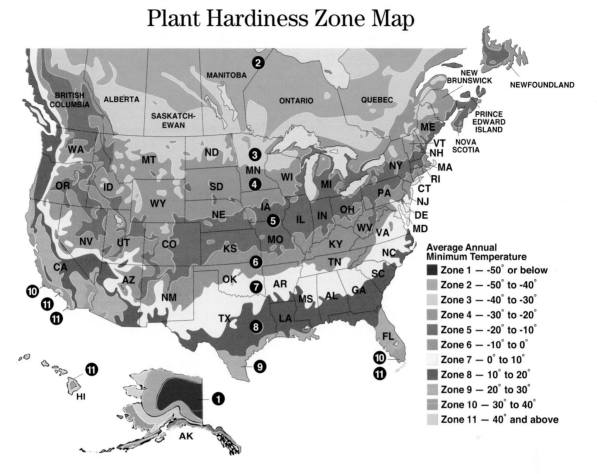

Average Annual
Minimum Temperature

Zone 1 — -50° or below
Zone 2 — -50° to -40°
Zone 3 — -40° to -30°
Zone 4 — -30° to -20°
Zone 5 — -20° to -10°
Zone 6 — -10° to 0°
Zone 7 — 0° to 10°
Zone 8 — 10° to 20°
Zone 9 — 20° to 30°
Zone 10 — 30° to 40°
Zone 11 — 40° and above

Plant Heat Zone Map

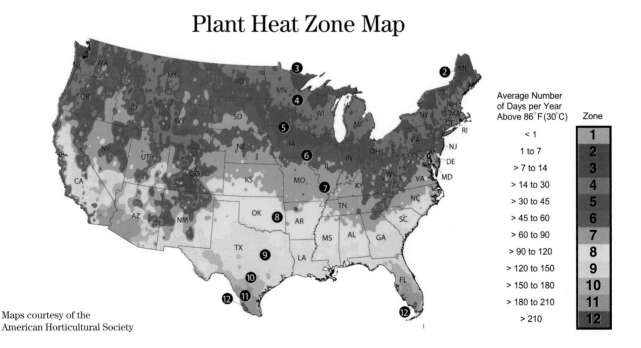

Average Number of Days per Year Above 86°F (30°C)	Zone
< 1	1
1 to 7	2
> 7 to 14	3
> 14 to 30	4
> 30 to 45	5
> 45 to 60	6
> 60 to 90	7
> 90 to 120	8
> 120 to 150	9
> 150 to 180	10
> 180 to 210	11
> 210	12

Maps courtesy of the
American Horticultural Society

Index

Index

"Every single story that
nature tells is gorgeous."
—*Natalie Angier*